READING AND THE

PSYCHOLOGY OF PERCEPTION

❖

Hunter Diack

GREENWOOD PRESS, PUBLISHERS
WESTPORT, CONNECTICUT

ACKNOWLEDGMENTS

I cannot put this book before the public without acknowledging the stimulus and help I have received. First, I must mention Professor M. M. Lewis, Director of the University of Nottingham, Institute of Education. Not only was he generous in the time and attention he gave to the discussion of many of the ideas now assembled in this book, but I am indebted also to him for the help I found in his book, *Infant Speech*.

The debt I owe to my colleague, J. C. Daniels, is incalculable. Most of the ideas specifically connected with reading which appear in this book have been threshed out in argument and discussion with him. The high degree of agreement between us has been evident in other writings. Any differences we have had in this field have in the main been differences of emphasis. My debt to him is particularly evident in the section on *Progress in Reading*. The statistics in that publication were his work. But I must absolve him from any responsibility for the selection and treatment of the statistical facts in the section referred to.

Miss C. E. Land, Librarian of the Institute, was generous in her help in finding references and in keeping me informed as to the pertinent work on the topic I was concerned with. In various ways other members of the Institute staff were helpful.

It is impossible for me to list by name the large number of teachers and parents, particularly in the Nottingham area, but also in other parts of England, Scotland, and South Africa, who put themselves to some trouble to supply me with information.

My final acknowledgment is to the children who taught me so much and to whom I dedicate this book.

Nottingham.
September, 1959.   HUNTER DIACK.

CONTENTS

Part One

THE RISE AND FALL

OF

GESTALT THEORY

Chapter I

WHY THIS BOOK WAS WRITTEN

This book evolved out of (a) a study of the development of language in the child during which it had become clear that a study of linguistic development was inextricably linked with the development of the perceptual powers, (b) researches which I had been engaged in with J. C. Daniels, my colleague at the University of Nottingham Institute of Education. These researches had been concerned with various aspects of the teaching of reading and as we pursued these researches I became more and more convinced that one of the important things to be done in this field was to re-state some of the facts about the perception of words and to investigate the part Gestalt psychology had played in the evolution of modern methods of teaching reading. These convictions arose because so many of the statements in the literature on reading contradicted my own observations and these statements very often bore traces of Gestalt influence, for example, in Schonell and elsewhere, I read that children found it difficult to distinguish between words of similar length or shape and yet I found that a three-year-old child learned to match sixteen three-letter words in thirteen minutes, and that many children on entering school could do so in as little time as it took to place the matching cards in the right position.

Another factor which led me to write this study was the continued acceptance of Gestalt theory by so many educational psychologists for so long after the theory had fallen into disrepute.

Gestalt theory has been interpreted by most of those who have written on the subject of reading as having the implication that children see 'words as wholes'. The phrase is ambiguous and becomes more ambiguous when it is expressed as 'seeing whole words'. For this reason

11

I have, like some other writers in this field, used the term 'word-whole' when I refer to the theory of reading based on Gestalt psychology. By this means the idea of 'wholeness' in perception is more adequately emphasised.

Books on the theory and method of teaching children to read abound in references to Gestalt theory. Some of these references are direct, others bring in Gestalt concepts by implication. In general it may be said that any writer who uses such terms as 'seeing words as wholes' or 'total word-pattern' is writing within the context of Gestalt theory as he has interpreted it. The following quotations are typical.

> We tend to see the whole pattern before we see the parts of it. A young child may recognise the word 'elephant' long before he knows the component letters. It is a distinctive 'word-pattern' . . . This tendency to see in 'wholes' is emphasized in the Gestalt hypothesis.
>
> DUNCAN, JOHN: *Backwardness in Reading.* 1953.

> The first obvious factor in the recognition of a word is its total pattern . . . we are causing unnecessary difficulties for the child in its first stages if we pack his reading vocabulary with too large a number of similar word-patterns . . . In addition to the whole pattern of the word particular letters in words have perceptual values for young children.
>
> SCHONELL, F. J.: *Backwardness in the Basic Subjects.* 1940.

> The whole-word method, which was advocated by Comenius in the seventeenth century, is based also (i.e. in addition to meaningfulness) on the idea that a word is more than the sum of its constituent letters. It has a visual and aural pattern of its own besides being invested with meaning. In recent years the idea has had considerable support from Gestalt psychologists, who claim that we tend to perceive wholes rather than parts of the whole.
>
> MURRAY, W. and DOWNES, C. W.: *Children Learn to Read.* 1955.

> Accurate visual recognition is fostered through attention first to the total form of word and later to details such as capital letters and inflectional endings . . . Differences in the configuration of words of the same length should be stressed.
>
> WITTY, P.: *Reading in Modern Instruction.* 1949.

Some children require careful guidance in establishing control over the cues to differences in word forms. First, the teacher should call attention to the differences in the configuration, or total shape of words . . . she may call attention to differences in the lengths of words by drawing a straight line frame around each word. This demonstration may be followed by an informal pupil discussion of the differences between the lengths of other pairs of words.

BETTS, E. A.: *Foundations of Reading Instruction*. 1950.

These quotations do not belong to the distant past, as the dates show. Though Gestalt theory reached its peak of reputation in the 1930's, the book from which the Murray and Downes quotation comes was published as recently as 1955. Only this year (1959) there appeared *Reading in the Modern Infants School* by Norah C. Goddard in which it was stated that one of the three really important discoveries which modern educational psychology has made is that children recognise words as wholes before they know the letters of the alphabet. In writing this she was merely relaying the echoes of scores of writers who have used half-truths as belaying pins in their climb into the clouds. Modern educational psychology did *not* 'discover' that children recognise words as wholes before they know the letters. That they do so was known and recognised before educational psychology was even a name. But what in this context does 'recognise' mean? What is the process behind the label?

Until those questions are answered, this commonplace of the literature on reading is no more than an irritating example of how, in the pseudo-scientific chit-chat that so often passes for authoritative advice to teachers, half-truths are treated as whole truths and casual observations gradually acquire the status of fully accredited scientific facts. Behind the statement that children recognise words as wholes lies a massive cloud of authority emanating from various interpretations of Gestalt theory.

For upwards of thirty years writers on the teaching of reading have leaned upon Gestalt theory. They have continued to do so even after the Gestalt system of thought has crumbled under logical analysis supported by more precise experimental work than any carried out by the founders of Gestalt theory.

Chapter II

WHAT IS A GESTALT?

In order to assess the contribution that Gestalt psychology really made to the development of reading theory I found it necessary in the first place to examine Gestalt theory itself. In the first part of this book I try to give those readers who have neither time nor opportunity to read the original literature a reasonably concise idea of what the Gestalt psychologists were trying to say in so far as it can be thought to be relevant to the teaching of reading. Most text-books of educational psychology do contain general summaries of Gestalt theory, but the only book I know which makes any attempt to assess the contribution of Gestalt theory to the teaching of reading is the recent *Reading—Chaos and Cure* by Terman and Walcutt (McGraw Hill, 1959).

It is by no means easy to give a concise account of what the Gestalt psychologists said. They said so many things and not always the same things. The Danish psychologist, Petermann, had this feeling thirty years ago when he set out to write a critical appraisal of Gestalt thinking. He had not gone very far in this enterprise before he discovered that what he should have to do was to write a history of the development of Gestalt ideas for he found no precise system of thought in Gestalt theory to which the tools of logical analysis could be applied. His comments were mild and academic. 'Gestalt literature is by no means homogeneous in its thought' he wrote in his book *Gestalt Theory* (1929) and this is a considerable understatement for a man who had found so little consistency in the theory that he was forced to write a different book from the one he had set out to do.

In spite of Petermann's testimony, Gestalt psychology continued to exert great influence upon educational thought. It was as though

Petermann had never written his book, for it was in the years following its publication that this school of psychology was at the height of its influence in the field of education. Fortunately the limits set by the aim of this present study make the task of giving a succinct criticism of Gestalt theory easier than that which confronted Petermann. In the mass of words with which the Gestalt psychologists flooded the learned journals there were a few particular ideas which made a special appeal to educationists. These few ideas also lie at the very root of the Gestalt theory.

The first of these is the idea of the Gestalt itself. In the language of ordinary life in Germany the word *Gestalt* means 'form' or 'pattern'—the shape that things have. The term began to have a special meaning in the psychological field as early as the 1870's when an Austrian psychologist, Von Ehrenfels, used the term 'Gestalt-qualität' when he was investigating the problem of how it was that a melody remained recognisably the same even when played in two different keys—every note was different but the melody was not thereby altered beyond easy recognition. During the last three decades of the nineteenth century there was a great deal of interest in this type of problem: How were the parts related to the whole? Some of the experiments carried out in the nineties are of particular interest in connection with the subject of this book. They were concerned with the perception of words. J. McK. Cattell using brief-exposure techniques reached the conclusion that the 'general shapes' of words were an important factor in the recognition of them and two other experimenters, Erdmann and Dodge, showed that in certain circumstances a whole word could be accurately perceived from a distance at which it was impossible for separate letters to be distinguished. The words were the 'wholes', the letters were the parts. There is a clear connection here with the work of von Ehrenfels whose problem was that the 'whole' (the melody) was heard to be the same though each one of the 'parts' (the notes) was changed. The same kind of phenomenon is encountered in the ordinary cinema. Each 'part' of a film is a still shot and yet the 'whole' that we see is a moving picture. It was indeed in studying the perception of motion that Wertheimer began to formulate the ideas that later developed into Gestalt psychology. In 1912 he published his paper on the perception of movement in the *Zeitschrift für Psychologie* and in that year also he delivered a lecture to the Kant Society of Berlin which is generally taken to be the first manifesto of the Gestalt School. In that lecture he defined a

Gestalt as 'a whole the behaviour of which is not determined by that of its individual elements but where the part-processes are themselves determined by the intrinsic nature of the whole'. In this lecture, too, he stated that the aim of Gestalt theory was nothing more or less than to determine the nature of such wholes. Referring to this occasion, Petermann pointed out that writers of the Gestalt School had declared quite explicitly that in that lecture the essentials of the new psychology were already formulated 'with entire definiteness' and that later experiment and writing added nothing to the framework of principles which Wertheimer then erected. The reader acquainted with psychological writing today, if he reads Wertheimer's lecture in, say, Ellis's *Source-Book of Gestalt Psychology*, will be surprised at this claim, for apart from the definition of Gestalt he will probably find nothing there except an attack upon what Wertheimer called 'atomistic' or 'brick-and-mortar' thinking. Katz, a later adherent of the Gestalt school, admitted that much of the earlier Gestalt writings were polemical rather than scientific and this is true of Wertheimer's manifesto.

The nineteenth century associationist psychologists had worked on the theory that knowledge was acquired piece-meal through experience: one accumulated knowledge part by part and thus built it up into a whole. Such a theory, if rigidly adhered to, could readily be thought of as in conflict with Wertheimer's notion of the predominance of the whole and certainly Wertheimer and his colleagues, Köhler and Koffka, made the most of the conflict. Catch-phrases quickly began to appear in the writings of the Gestalt psychologists, e.g. 'the whole is more than the sum of its parts', a phrase which is frequently echoed in the literature on reading to indicate that a word is more than a series of letters strung together. The neologism 'and-summation' was also invented, usually with the derogatory epithet 'mere' attached to it. 'Mere and-summation' meant adding together in an 'and, and, and' sort of way the part-processes. The implication was that this method of approach would not lead to the discovery of the essential nature of wholes which according to Wertheimer and his colleagues it was the aim of all research to discover.

Even if one admits that in their inquiry into the nature of wholes, the Gestalt psychologists were tackling an important problem, it is extremely difficult to find a precise meaning for the term Gestalt; it is the melody as distinct from the notes; it is the moving film as distinct from the stills. But where does one stop? It is the tree as distinct from the leaves; the ocean as distinct from the salt which is part of it; the shower of rain as distinct from the drops forming it; the molecule as distinct from the particles of energy composing it.

The moving picture exists in the mind, not in the stills. Is this what distinguishes the 'Gestalt' from these other 'wholes'? Not according to Köhler who wrote a paper called 'Physical Gestalten' in which he attempted to show that the Gestalt was a phenomenon of the physical world. One of the examples he gave was that of the charged conductor. It is impossible, Köhler pointed out, to change the potential on *part* of a charged surface 'any change produces a reaction through the entire natural structure'.

But is there any 'natural structure' of which a similar statement might not be made? Lop a branch of a tree and gradually the tree's direction of growth will change. In the case of the charged conductor the reaction takes place in an infinitesimal fraction of time, but this does not affect the principle.

On the other hand if a handful of peas is dropped on a table, if we disregard the infinitesimal magnetic attraction between such small bodies, there is no intrinsic relationship between the separate peas. It is possible, however, that three of these peas have landed in such a way as to form a neat triangle. Let one of these three peas be removed and the groupings in which we perceive the other peas will be affected. Yet the removal of the pea had no effect upon the other peas. What therefore was a 'mere and-summation', a random distribution of peas on a flat surface, was in fact 'structurally' perceived.

It may well be argued that Köhler's attempt to 'derive a physical Gestalt' was abortive and away from the main line of development. Yet it does strikingly illustrate how all-inclusive the Gestalt psychologists were prepared to make their central term. Most of their experimental work was concerned with optical illusions and this indicates that they habitually thought of the Gestalt as being 'mental' as opposed to physical.

17

Chapter III

UNLEARNED SEEING

In a series of Third Programme talks in which a series of different speakers dealt with various aspects of contemporary experimental psychology, a Cambridge psychologist, A. F. Watson, gave an account of Gestalt psychology in which occurred this paragraph:

> On the basis of the illusion experiments I have mentioned, together, with many others, Gestalt psychologists have felt themselves justified in claiming generally that from infancy, we perceive the world in the complex, fully articulated way that we do as adults. That is to say, that they regard our perception as being independent of any previous learning: I may be expected, for instance, to pick out the difference between a triangle and a square upon the very first occasion on which I am presented with these figures. What I see will be determined solely by the innate construction of my visual receiving system and the relevant stimuli. This doctrine they expressed by the term 'innate organisation of perception'.

It is perhaps surprising that anyone should seriously claim that infants perceive things in the same fully articulated way as adults and more surprising that the claim should have been taken seriously. I have considerable doubts as to whether Watson himself really understood what that fully articulated way was and should imagine that if asked about the phrase he would have replied that whether it was understood or not it was as near as he could get to a statement of the Gestalt view of this matter and that it was at the very least an accurate echo of some of the statements made by Gestalt writers.

There has, however, been about as much confusion in dealing with 'experience' as with the concept of the Gestalt itself. In what sense could it possibly be maintained that a child of two looking at a starry sky can see it in 'the fully articulated way' of an astronomer?

If the term Gestalt shed so much of its meaning by the sheer extension of its application, the term 'perceive' as the Gestalt writers used it lost as much of its meaning by the limitations the Gestalt school placed upon it. They wrote as though visual perception was a matter in which only the visual sense was concerned. This is to say, when the light-sensitive cells of the retinae were stimulated by the light reflected by a triangular shape, then there necessarily occurred in the brain a series of psycho-physical events correlated with triangular shape. These events occurred naturally, spontaneously, immediately. This being so, there would be no need for a human being to see a triangle twice before the psycho-physical events correlated with triangular shapes occurred in his brain. Having been committed to the theory of a direct relationship between the stimulus object and the mental events stimulated by it, the Gestalt psychologists found themselves also committed to denying to past experience the vital role which ordinary commonsense has always attributed to it.

Gottschaldt.

One of the Gestalt psychologists who worked hard at the task of showing that 'previous experience' was not so important after all was Gottschaldt. His paper on this subject is given in full in Ellis's *Source-Book*.

Gottschaldt worked from the hypothesis: "If 'experience' theories are correct, then the more frequently a certain figure has been presented the easier it should be to apprehend *this* figure when it appears in a larger one". The following are examples of the type of figures he used.

(*a*)

19

(b)

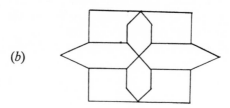

Five figures of type (a) were presented one at a time to two groups of students by means of an episcope projection lantern. The presentations lasted one second and there were three-second intervals between them. Group One saw each figure three times. Group Two saw each figure 520 times. In order to keep the subjects ignorant of the real purpose of the experiment, the instructions were to memorize the figures so that they could be drawn later from memory. After this 'memorizing' series had been completed, five corresponding figures of type (b) were shown one at a time to the subjects with an exposure of two seconds each and they were asked to describe in detail anything that particularly attracted their attention in the figures.

The result of this experiment was that there was no marked difference between the two groups in the number of times the 'learned' (a) figures stood out within the pattern of the (b) figures. An increase of 24 per cent. in the number of times this happened, however, occurred in *both* groups when they were given instructions to search for the (a) figures in the (b) figures, so again there was no significant difference in the performance of the two groups. It is note-worthy that Group One consisted of only three students and Group Two of only eight. The figures illustrated are among the easier items in the series of tests. In this case it would seem that all that needed to be learned through 'past experience' was learned after the three presentations only and the members of the group who were shown the figure 520 times learned no more during the 517 presentations that remained. Other figures were much more difficult, e.g.

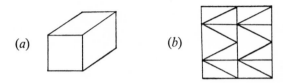

(a)   (b)

and these would appear to have had the opposite effect. The (a) figures were so obscured by the details of the (b) figures that even after 520 presentations many of the subjects could not disentangle them.

Few experiments that have been taken seriously can have been so naive. Gottschaldt simply did not seem to be aware that with the simple figures there was nothing more to be learned after the first three presentations or that with the more complicated ones the problems were in general too difficult to be solved within the conditions of the experiment. Nor did he seem to be aware that in deliberately misleading his subjects as to the aim of the experiment, he was begging the question he was attempting to answer. In deliberately depriving the subjects of the real purpose of the experiment, he was assuming that the 'experience' of knowing what they were really given to be tested in would affect the quality of their perception and at the same time was unconsciously 'rigging' the experiment in order to show that 'experience' did not have this effect.

These weaknesses, unfortunately, since he was unaware of them, did not prevent him from some imposing philosophising. He claimed to have shown that past experience does not constitute 'an independent force capable of modifying subsequent perception in a specific manner' and there is such an air of philosophical authority in the following paragraph that it is perhaps not surprising that students of psychology, who frequently owing to pressure of time skip the descriptions of the experiments and rely on the conclusions, were taken in by it:

> Since our findings indicate that there are at all events *some* cases where 'past experience' (in the sense of bare repetition) is practically without effect, it follows that important changes must be made in 'experience theory' itself. Any appeal to 'past experience' as an explanatory concept must limit itself in one or other of the following ways. The theory may renounce any claim to universal validity and indicate instead its own range of application, in which case a reformulation of the entire concept seems inevitable. Or if the claim to universality is maintained, the admission must be made that the degree of such influences is in many cases well-nigh negligible in comparison with other factors. And it would then be these other factors (apart from the influence of instruction and other subjectively induced factors) which would play the principal roles. The influence of such forces is not dependent upon 'past experience' with the object in question, but depends rather upon the organisational conditions of the perceptual field itself; these forces are determined by the *intrinsic* properties of the stimulus object not by such contingent conditions as those postulated by 'experience theory'.

It is Koffka who most clearly and most acceptably expresses the 'configurational' view with regard to the role of experience. This view, he states, 'assumes that a certain order dominates experience from the beginning'. He adds that this view brings the Gestalt school in conflict with current views which 'assume that order comes only as a result of experience'.

Different 'Experiences'.

This conflict between Gestalt views and those which Koffka calls 'current' is the key to understanding why Gestalt writers expressed themselves as they did about 'experience'. A great deal of their writing is plain revolt against crude associationist theory which they sometimes referred to as 'experience theory' or simply 'experience'. We can see this happening quite strikingly in another passage by Koffka. He is discussing the development of the powers of perception in very young children.

> Yet the child recognises its mother's face as early as the second month and in the middle of the first year the reaction to a 'friendly' face is quite different to the reaction to an 'angry' face. Furthermore, this difference is of a kind which obliges us to conclude that 'friendly' and 'angry' faces are phenomenal facts to the infant, and

not mere distributions of light and shade. It seems quite impossible to explain this behaviour by experience . . .

If I interrupt the quotation at this point, the reader may well be somewhat nonplussed, because though the term 'experience' may not of itself carry an *explanation* with it, it certainly does look as though Koffka were leading up to the statement which suggests that experience as we normally conceive it had nothing to do with the developing of the child's perceptual powers between the second month and the middle of the first year. If I now continue the quotation, it becomes clear that he is using the term 'experience' in a special way. The rest of the sentence is in apposition to 'by experience':

. . . upon the assumption that these phenomena arise from an original chaos of sensations in which single visual sensations combine with one another, together with unpleasant or pleasant consequences.

Wertheimer in *Untersuchungen zur Lehre der Gestalt* had put the same point somewhat differently:

When we are presented with a number of different stimuli, we do not as a rule experience a number of individual things, this one and that and that. Instead, larger wholes separated from and related to one another are given in experience: their arrangement and division are concrete and definite.

What Wertheimer and his school were greatly concerned to do, therefore, was to put forward a contrary hypothesis to that of the associationists, following on the work of von Ehrenfels, Benussi, and Husserl.

Koffka based his explanation of 'innate organisation' on the 'figure-ground hypothesis' of Rubin which, simply expressed, means no more than that objects are never seen in isolation but always as figures arising out of a background. The babe-in-arms, for example, who by his actions shows that he has 'seen' a bright point of light could not, according to Rubin, be accurately be said merely to have seen the point of light but to have seen it and its darker background as well.

In making use of this hypothesis Koffka stated that the first phenomena were *'qualities* or *figures upon a ground'*. But he went on

23

to say that it is only the simplest of mental configurations that are independent of experience. Discrimination between even such simple figures as triangles and squares is possible, according to him, only as a result of learning.

This is a very different view from that which we have seen put forward by Gottschaldt. In meeting such inconsistencies within the school one begins to feel a great deal of sympathy with Petermann in his failure to find a consistently solid basis for the writing of a logical critique of Gestalt theory.

Wertheimer drew up a series of laws of Gestalt formation. These laws are usually listed in the descriptions of Gestalt psychology. The 'law' to which least attention is paid is the 'law of experience'. Yet there it is in Wertheimer's list, a 'law' which in effect states that perceptual experience leads to modifications of perceptual experience— the opposite of what Gottschaldt was so determined to prove.

Chapter IV

" AHA ! "

The third major concept of the Gestalt school is that denoted by the term 'insight'—'the "Aha!" of the Gestalt psychologists'. It was Köhler's treatment of this concept in *The Mentality of Apes* which brought it to the forefront in Gestalt theory. Later in *Gestalt Psychology* he complained that some readers of the earlier work had not quite understood what he had intended to convey by the term. They had wrongly 'interpreted this formulation as though it referred to a mysterious mental agent or faculty which was made responsible for the apes' behaviour'. He went on then to explain that by 'insight' he meant no more than 'awareness of determination' by which he meant 'awareness of what was determined a particular event' or, as one would put it in simpler English, 'awareness of causes'. He went on to give an example.

He is in a concert hall and finds himself in an attitude of admiring. The object of his admiration is an alto voice. He has, he says, direct experience of this causal relationship.

> I needed no indirect criteria, no scientific investigations, no co-efficients of correlation, in order to know about the connection between the singing and my admiration. As a matter of fact, my experience told me more than any scientific induction could. For induction is silent as to the nature of the functional relation which it predicates, while in the present example a particular fact of psychological causation was directly experienced as an understandable relationship.

This later treatment of the concept of insight, however, does seem to be in some measure an abnegation of his former views since in the *The Mentality of Apes* he emphasised, or at least appeared to emphasise, the dramatic suddenness with which the insight arrives. In

Gestalt Psychology he appears to be saying no more than that we know many things intuitively. His earlier description, however, is more characteristic of Gestalt thinking generally. Wertheimer, in *Drei Abhandlungen zur Gestalt Theorie* frequently emphasises the suddenness of the arrival of insight: it arrives with a 'click'. He gives a number of examples, of which this is one:

A lawyer is in the habit of destroying the papers of cases so many years back. Consequently the records of Case A were recently burned. One day he is looking for a certain receipt connected with a current Case K. It cannot be found. Suddenly he recalls that the *contents* of the receipt had to do with Case A—and the A papers have been destroyed!

'The ordinary working of logic does not suffice here', Wertheimer adds, 'in addition there must be a 'click' so to speak, which snaps them together into the kind of inner relationship which *is* the conclusion'.

In spite of Köhler's part-withdrawal, therefore, one must take it that in general the Gestalt psychologists have associated insight not with mere awareness of relationships but with the kind of awareness that comes in a flash. The readers of whom Köhler complained were in fact not quite so wrong as he would have us believe.

It is not the suddenness with which the insight arrives that is important, however, but rather the fact that this very suddenness is taken to imply that it is something which does not come about according to the ordinary rules of logic.

Here is Wertheimer on this topic:

For a moment the premises are side by side, then suddenly there is a 'click' . . . the whole concept undergoes a complete reorganisation . . . traditional logic is suitable only for one who already knows everything and needs only a system of classification. For a genuine advance in knowledge it is useless.

Where then may we expect a genuine advance of knowledge to come from? Wertheimer leaves us in no doubt about that. From the earliest days he had been advocating the need for seeing problems 'as a whole'. He had for long been advocating the need for attacking problems 'from above' and not as science was in the habit of doing 'from below'. By 'from below' Wertheimer meant beginning with the elements of a situation and adding them up in a 'brick-and-mortar' sort of way: by 'from above' he meant seeing the whole structure and examining the elements in the light of it. This attack on traditional logic was written in the 1920's. Twenty years later Wertheimer was writing the posthumously published *Productive Thinking*. In this book he gave a series of brief histories of the solutions of problems beginning with simple problems first and showing how 'rote' learners and 'insight' learners would set about their solution, and concluding with a description of the steps by which Einstein evolved the theory of relativity.

Wertheimer claimed to have demonstrated by means of these commentaries on how problems are solved that there are processes of thought that are 'genuine, fine, clean, direct and productive'. This piling up of adjectives belongs more to the language of enthusiasm than of science or even philosophy. Wertheimer, however, went on to try to define the characteristics of this kind of thinking. Here in quotation and summary, is what he had to say:

In 'productive thinking' there are factors at work which 'traditional approaches' have neglected or been unaware of. 'These factors are related to whole characteristics, they function with reference to such characteristics, determined by structural requirements for a sensible situation'. That is to say the items, data, relations, etc., 'arise and function as parts in their place and role within the whole'. Traditional operations, e.g. analysis, generalisation, inference, forming syllogisms, etc., are still involved in productive thinking, but they too function in relation to whole characteristics. The productive processes are 'on the whole not of the character of an and-summation aggregation, of a succession of piecemeal, chance happenings in which items, associations, operations just occur'. In their development these processes often lead to sensible expectations, assumptions. These call for an honest attitude, for verifications. The situation calls not merely for piecemeal factual truth, it calls for 'structural truth'.

In thus summarising the characteristics of 'productive thinking' I have followed Wertheimer's text very closely and have included all the characteristics he tabulates.

According to Wertheimer a problem exists when one's picture of a situation is not fully 'structured' or 'Gestaltet'. He uses the symbol S_1 for the situation in which the actual thought process starts and S_2 for that in which the process ends, the problem having been solved. S_1 as compared with S_2 is structurally incomplete: it involves a gap or a

27

structural trouble. S_2 is 'sensibly complete' as against S_1.

When the problem is realised, S_1 contains structural strains and stresses that are resolved in S_2. The thesis is that the very character of the steps, of the operations, of the changes between S_1 and S_2 springs from the nature of the vectors set up in these structural troubles in the direction of helping the situation, of straightening it out structurally.

Two further paragraphs complete the picture of insight into problems as Wertheimer sees it.

It is interesting to compare the psychological situation in cases in which, after the problem is put and seen, and the subject does not know how to proceed, someone arrives with the ready-made solution. The subject may or may not understand it, may or may not realise that this is the solution; in any case, it was not reached by him, it did not come into existence in the realisation of the steps which are structurally required. It often gives him a shock, sometimes an unpleasant one. For real understanding one has to re-create the steps, the structural inner relatedness, the requiredness.

I repeat: the thesis is that the very structural features in S_2 with their particular, concrete nature create the vectors, in their direction, quality, intensity, that in turn lead to the steps and operations dynamically in line with the requirements. This development is determined by the so-called Prägnanz principle, by the tendencies to the good gestalt, by the various gestalt laws.

And so we find that the laws of Gestalt formation are extended to cover not only visual perception but also the operations of logic, a new Gestalt-based logic which is in some ways conflict with traditional logic.

28

Chapter V

A THEORY IN DECLINE

Gestalt theory was in its hey-day in the 'twenties and 'thirties. That a system of ideas as cloudy and confused as this ever had a hey-day at all may surprise any reader who has no more than a cursory acquaintance with the history of psychology. But it is in fact no more surprising than the rise of the behaviorist school of psychology which attempted to turn psychology into a science by deleting self-consciousness from the list of phenomena it was permissible to study and deciding that anything we learn by examining the workings of our own minds introspectively is not legitimate knowledge. If ever there was an attempt to produce *Hamlet* without the prince, this was it. Yet the production went on and indeed fulfilled a useful purpose in putting a curb on some of the wilder fantasies of psychologists generally.

The relationship between the academic world and the less specialised reading public is a very curious one. Academic writers like to think that their high-minded pursuit of the truth as they see it will eventually by its sheer quality come to influence the general thought of the day. No doubt this does happen in many fields. It is, I think, happening in the field of psychology at the present day. Three of the major schools of psychology that emerged during this century acquired their publics in a different manner, however. No one could surpass Freud in the production of recondite passages, but it was not this kind of writing which made him a name to conjure with but rather the highly coloured sexual fantasies he wove round people's dreams. The Behaviorist school came into prominence not through obscure papers in learned journals but through the hard-hitting, popularly written *Psychology from the Stand-Point of a Behaviorist* in which J. B. Watson hit out in a popular style at everyone who had even remotely entertained the idea that a system of psychology could be produced by sitting at a desk and thinking about what went on in one's own and other people's heads.

29

The book which gave Gestalt theory its most powerful thrust was without a doubt Köhler's *The Mentality of Apes*. This is a much more respectable book than Freud's *Interpretation of Dreams* and it had none of the bite and sting of Watson's best-seller. But there was drama in the circumstances in which the book was written and no book ever had a title better calculated to promote sales in the circumstances of the time. For by the time the book appeared on the market the war-mentality was being thought of as an ape-mentality, and here was a German intellectual who had spent the years of the only World War there had yet been interned on the island of Teneriffe studying the mentality of apes. Besides, it was a very good book. One did not have to be versed in the psychology of any school at all to be interested in this study of what appeared to be the glimmerings of a just sub-human intelligence. This book did more than any other to draw attention to the previous work of the Gestalt psychologists.

The dominant part that Gestalt theory played in psychological writings and the subsequent weakening of its influence are well illustrated by the following quotation from *A Further Study of Perception* (1956) by Professor M. D. Vernon:

In 1937 was published a book by the present author entitled *Visual Perception*, the principal aim of which was to collect and collate systematically the main psychological experiments on that subject, their results and conclusions. A considerable part of the book was occupied by the work of the Gestalt psychologists. And although little or no exposition of the *Gestalt Theorie* was included, yet the outlook and the ingenious and extensive experimental material emanating from this school of psychology inevitably dominated the book, just as at that time it dominated the minds of those psychologists who were interested in the experimental approach to perceptual problems. Since then, the main trends of thought on these problems have changed their direction. The Gestalt psychologists, and especially Köhler, have turned increasingly to theoretical speculation as to the physical basis in the cerebral cortex of the perceptual processes. On the other hand, continued study by other psychologists inspired by the original work of the Gestalt school—for instance, on the 'constancies'—seem to have produced a mass of detailed results leading to conflicting conclusions, or to no conclusions at all. The apparently clear outlines originally drawn by the Gestalt psychologists have become blurred and dimmed. And it has seemed perhaps that their experimental results and their theories did not after all indicate a fundamental basis for the understanding of the nature of perception, but rather a one-sided exaggeration of certain features by no means the most important in perceiving as we ordinarily experience it.

Professor Vernon is one of the most skilful summarisers of experimental work. The reader who wishes to make himself acquainted with the experimental work upon which this changed view-point is based can do no better than consult this book.

The experiments of Senden are perhaps of particular interest. He experimented with human beings who had been blind from birth and had recovered their sight after surgical operations. Some of the subjects in these experiments were adults who had learned a great deal about the shapes of things through the sense of touch. Yet they were astonishingly slow in learning to discriminate by sight between such simple figures as squares and circles. In some cases discrimination between shapes of that simple nature was achieved only after several laborious weeks. Experiments of this kind appeared to provide very conclusive evidence that any Gestalt psychologist who claimed that perception owed nothing or little to previous experience were very far from the truth. And yet the proof was not really water-tight. Was there not a possibility of degeneration of the visual nerve-cells through lack of use? Was it not possible that the abnormal use of the tactile centre of the brain had produced some kind of blockage in the visual centre? Objections of this kind were made, legitimately enough. Those who made them, however, were often using them in arguments in favour of unlearned perception. Yet to argue that tactile experience may create a visual blockage is to admit the influence of past experience.

As recently as 1951, Lashley, one of the most famous of American neurologists, with a team of co-workers, reported a series of experiments which turned out to be critical of Gestalt theory as it had by then developed. This was a particularly interesting turn of events because the experiments through which Lashley had chiefly acquired fame had led him to emphasise the 'whole functioning' of the brain. These earlier experiments did not place him among the ranks of the Gestalt psychologists, but they could be said to have indicated that he had a certain sympathy with the Gestalt point of view. What he and his co-workers were interested in, in the experiments reported in 1951, was the validity of Köhler's theory of 'field excitations', that elaborate theory referred to in the quotation from Professor Vernon above.

Köhler's theory of 'field excitations' is the result of complicated speculation about the physical events that occur in the brain during perception. It is an extension of the traditional isomorphism of Gestalt theory, i.e. the belief that there is a direct relationship between what happens in the brain and the object perceived. This does not mean that when we see a triangle there is a triangle of excitation in the brain. Even Köhler would not drive his speculations to that length, though one has a feeling that he wished he could. What he did maintain, however, was that when an object was perceived there occurred in the brain a field of excitation which was correlated in some way with the object perceived. It would seem to follow that if the field of excitation correlated with a particular object were to be disturbed then either the object would not be recognised at all or would be perceived as something else. An interesting field for speculation or for a Wellsian fantasy! This was the assumption on which Lashley and his co-workers based their experiments. Having taught a few rhesus monkeys to recognise particular objects, they then operated on the animals inserting gold pins and gold leaf strips into the visual areas of the cortex. They assumed that the metal pins and strips would short-circuit some of the nerve-currents and thus distort the fields of excitation and, if Köhler's theory were correct, this would result in a distortion of perception. These monkeys, however, showed no sign of having distorted perception. After they recovered from the operation, they were no worse at recognising the objects than before. The experimenters thereupon came to the conclusion that the theory, though ingenious, was inadequate.

In discussing the significance of their experiment they also pointed out that 'field theory' ignored 'the selective action of habits and set'— which is a roundabout way of saying that past experience has more influence upon present perception than Gestalt theory, even as modified by Köhler's later speculations, was willing to admit.

Philosophy Too.

It is not only in the experimental field that Gestalt theory has been attacked in recent years. It has also been attacked at the philosophical level. In an article in *Mind* Professor Hamlyn argued in detail that a discussion of Gestalt theory necessarily becomes a discussion of the meaning of terms. The earlier pages of this study suggest that this is so but also suggest that the discussion would have been better carried out by the Gestalt writers themselves before they let so much vague speculation loose upon the world. In that article in *Mind*, Hamlyn took up that commonplace of Gestalt literature—'the whole is more than the sum of its parts' and argued that either nothing is more than the sum of its parts or else everything must be according to how one is using one's terms. This is very much the conclusion reached in my earlier discussion of the term 'Gestalt' when it was shown that the difficulty is not in discovering what is a Gestalt but rather in finding anything that is not one.

The following quotation from the same author's *Psychology of Perception*, wholly devoted to a criticism of Gestalt theory, will give an idea of the temper of the criticism which Hamlyn handed out to Gestalt psychology in his book. In the section from which the quotation is taken he is dealing with Rubin's figure-ground hypothesis, the hypothesis which Koffka used as the basis of his version of Gestalt theory.

> These ideas hardly deserve the dignity of 'figure-ground hypothesis'—for, clearly, when we identify an object we must distinguish it from everything else which forms its background. What we *mean* by an object is something which can be so distinguished and it would not make sense to talk of our seeing an object which was not so distinguished. Thus to call it a 'hypothesis' is at the least misleading . . .
>
> To say that the tendency to distinguish figure and ground is innate is also misleading, for the truth is that if we are to see an object at all, it is a logical necessity that we must distinguish it from a background. This is not contingent and therefore not a matter of experience. Perceiving something involves identifying it, and identifying it involves distinguishing it from other things. *But* to say that if we see an object at all is not a matter of experience that we have come to distinguish it from a background is not the same as saying that the figure-ground distinction is innately given . . . the thesis that the figure-ground distinction is innate suggests that the baby is born making such distinctions and this is unlikely. It is certainly true that we are born with the *capacity* for learning to distinguish objects, on the other hand, and once we do we see them against a background as a logical necessity.

Gibson in *The Perception of the Visual World* is a much more sympathetic critic of the Gestalt view. His work developed from his war-time task of training pilots to see accurately and in a well-orientated manner during high-speed flight. In his book he pointed out that the Gestalt psychologists devoted their energies to answering a subsidiary question in the field of perception. Their laws of sensory organisation explain—'if they do explain'—why the perceived form differs from the retinal form. In Gibson's view the fundamental question is the opposite of this.

We require to know not why optical illusions occur but why on normal occasions they do not occur. We require to know why the cortical events correspond to the retinal events not why they fail to do so. His main suggestions, supported by a considerable amount of acute thinking, were that 'the ordinal distribution' of the points of stimulation on the retina is itself a stimulus and that it is to this ordinal stimulus that the cortical events correspond. As I understand this, he means that if, say, there falls upon the retinae an image of three dots, these dots constitute at the very minimum four stimuli. Each dot is itself a stimulus, but the spatial relational of the points of stimulation on the retinae is also a stimulus. These ordinal stimuli produce 'psycho-physical correlates' in the brain. Gibson emphasises the term *correlates* indicating that the cortical events are *correlated with*, not *copies of* the retinal stimulation. Gibson was of the opinion that in this way he had shown Köhler's elaborate theory of 'cortical fields' to be unnecessary and had at the same time shown that it was unnecessary to assume that 'interpretive mental acts' invariably accompanied acts of visual perception. Gibson works out his theory in a fascinating book. The great weakness of it is, however, that like the more orthodox Gestalt psychologists he paid too little attention to the effect of experience upon perception. Only in the most cursory manner does he refer to the fact that what we have learned about an object influences the manner in which we perceive it.

From Gestalt theory there has developed 'field psychology' in general. Since these later developments have not perceptibly influenced any theory of teaching reading, they do not concern us in this study. Experts in reading have been content to select what suited them from the earlier commonplaces of the Gestalt school.

Chapter VI

A NEW LOOK AT PERCEPTION

What happens in the brain of an adult human being when he sees a familiar object and recognises it as such—an apple, let us say? It is not within the power of any psychologist, physiologist or neurologist to give a complete answer to the question. The verb 'see' is one of those simple little words that are exceedingly deceptive because the processes they stand for are so very complicated. They are certainly more complicated than the Gestalt psychologists appreciated.

In the first place it is quite clear that what happens in the brain is not merely a series of psycho-physical events occurring in the visual centre of the cortex; it is not *merely* a 'visual image'. This may be the sort of mental activity characteristic of imbeciles, the ordinary adult human being, however, has a much richer response. Whenever he consciously sees, say, an apple, he is likely to say to himself in sub-vocal speech the word 'apple'. This means that in his brain there occur events analogous to those which would occur if he said the word aloud. In learning to say a word meaningfully several of the brain-centres are involved. When the adult as a child learned to say the word 'apple' with understanding, the visual centre was certainly involved; he saw the thing of which he was learning the name. The auditory centre was involved also, at least twice, for he had to hear the name before he could repeat it and he had to hear the sounds he himself made in his attempt to say the word otherwise he would not

35

have known whether he had made the right sounds in the right order; the speech-motor centre was also involved because messages had to be sent to the speech-muscles; the kinaesthetic sense was involved too, because one necessarily *feels* the position and movements of lips, larynx, and tongue, and so also with the muscles of the eyes. As his understanding of the word 'apple' increased through experience of apples, other brain centres became involved—the centres concerned with touch, smell and taste. As his experience developed still more, he may have acquired a vast store of knowledge about apples, knowledge, for example, which would enable him to say at a glance what variety of apple he was looking at. I am not suggesting that every time a man sees an apple he relives the whole history of the word as he has experienced it. What actually happens in any person's brain will vary from one occasion to the next. A man who is very hungry and thirsty trudging past an orchard on a very hot day will have very different things happening in his mind when he sees the apples on the trees compared with those which occurred when a dish of apples was passed to him at the end of a substantial meal. Different though the two sets of events may be, however, they are both related to his past experience of apples. It is in fact impossible for an ordinary human being to 'see' an apple or anything else in the way the Gestalt psychologists sometimes maintained, often hoped, and nearly always assumed. It is not possible for the *conscious* visual perception of an object to take place without (a) the involvement of past experience, (b) the involvement of other centres besides the visual.

Because the Gestalt psychologists so greatly under-estimated the role of past experience—in spite of having a 'law of experience'—and because they habitually wrote as though visual perception was almost entirely a matter of the visual sense, they were not writing about characteristically human perception at all. Their main concern was to establish that a certain order prevailed from the beginning in the world-as-perceived, the 'organisation' being part of the natural functioning of the organs of perception. This is not a characteristic of human beings as distinct from other creatures, and indeed provided the terms in which the idea was expressed had been kept within logical bounds, there could be no substantial argument against it. We do, of course, 'tend to see wholes'. In certain respects we quite clearly do not have to *learn* to see. These unlearned perceptions do arrive, as it were, already packaged, in 'whole' form and do not have to be built up

36

on a basis of past experience in a 'brick-and-mortar' sort of way. One easy example shows that there can be no possible doubt about the truth of this basic Gestalt position: an infant has to learn to *read* a picture in the sense of requiring past experience of real things and of pictures before he can say that such and such a picture is, say, a picture of a dog, but he does not have to *learn* to organise the separate dots of printing ink of which the picture is composed. Nor does he have to *learn* to organise in a 'brick-and-mortar' sort of way the single dot of light flashing across the television screen and thus 'construct' the picture he sees. It is tempting to say that the sensory receiving mechanisms, do not respond to discrete, isolated stimuli but do respond to configurations of stimuli. There are, however, as so often in dealing with Gestalt theory, considerable semantic difficulties here.

Messages and Stimuli.

A stimulus is something which produces a response. A single, discrete stimulus would be one in which only one receptor cell was involved producing a response. In the case of the eye this is inconceivable. In the tiny foveal area of the eye alone there are many thousands of receptor cells and the retinal image of even so small an object as an apple may fall upon an area of the retina much greater than the foveal area. The response must therefore be not to one single message but to many thousands of messages. One cannot speak of any one of these messages, i.e. a message originating in one receptor cell as a stimulus without at the same time making the assumption that there is a response to that stimulus in isolation, an assumption which cannot be experimentally verified and which few people would care to make. What one can say, however, is that the sensory receiving mechanism is so constructed as to respond to configurations of messages.

Discussions of Gestalt theory have a tendency to get lost in epistemology. I myself find great difficulty in regarding a 'message' emanating from one receptor cell as a 'stimulus' when it cannot be shown to have a separate response, and I find it just as difficult to assume the necessity for 'interpretive mental acts' at the elementary levels of perception. There is no evidence that a fly has to learn to 'organise' or 'interpret' the many messages from its many-faceted eyes or that a tortoise has to *learn* to analyse the messages that are sent to

37

its brain from its beady eyes. In the *mere* fact of the organisation of perception it is not necessary to assume learning in any ordinary sense of the term. One is tempted to say that mere 'maturation' is enough and a great many writers have fallen before the temptation. This term, however, carries with it the suggestion that 'maturation' is something cut off and independent of experience and unfortunately most of those who have made use of the term have allowed this implication to carry greater weight than logic would have allowed.

What maturation can take place in the sense of sight of a baby without eyes? The optic nerves and visual centre may be anatomically perfect, but none of the ordinary events take place there. Without those elementary 'experiences', maturation on ordinary lines can hardly be expected to take place.

With the very stringent limitations suggested here, then, it is possible to accept the Gestalt thesis of the innate organisation of perception. The limitations are so restrictive, however, that the statement has very little bearing upon the facts of human perception. It is little more than a statement of the belief that when two or more parallel sets of events happen in the sensory receiving mechanism they affect one another. In what sense can it be said that a baby has to *learn* that the two sets of messages sent to its brain by its two separate eyes refer to one world? The owl gets two sets of messages about the same world; the chicken gets two sets of messages about different halves of the same world. At these elementary levels the term 'maturation' will do but only if used without the suggestion that it takes place regardless of experience.

It was a great mistake on the part of the Gestalt psychologists to take a principle that could be logically maintained with reference to the most elementary levels of perception and extend it far beyond these legitimate boundaries. Koffka, as we have seen was careful not to do so; Gottschaldt is an example at the other extreme. The general looseness of their writing gave it a strong leaning towards the Gottschaldt side, however. Even Gibson who denied the necessity for 'interpretive mental acts' was clearly not sufficiently aware of this weakness. Perception as it takes place in normal human life is scarcely separable from 'interpretive mental acts'—if the phrase means what the ordinary use of the words suggests. The fundamental 'interpretive mental act' is classification. Indeed it can scarcely be said that a thing is perceived by a human being unless it is *placed* in relation to other things and this is usually done by naming it in 'inner speech'? The

Gestalt psychologists, however, were remarkably consistent in their neglect of language and the part it plays in perception. It is necessary, however, in a critical assessment of Gestalt theory to consider rather carefully the role of language in perception.

Theory of the Analogue.

W. S. Morris, whose book *Signs, Language and Behavior* may well turn out to be a seminal one, found that loose language so greatly hindered clear discussion of psychological matters that a new vocabulary was necessary. He went a long way towards compiling one. I have in this study deliberately restricted the use of technical terms. In the cloud-bestrewn realms of psychology it is rather too easy to substitute pregnant-sounding terms for logical thought. So much so that there is no better principle for the writer of psychological books than 'Occam's razor': entities are not to be multiplied beyond what is necessary.

I found it necessary, however, to use one term in a rather special sense, an old term given a special meaning—the term *analogue*. This was necessary because the term *image* is unsatisfactory.

Gibson with his term 'psycho-physical correlates' appears to have been aware of at least one of the difficulties of the term 'image'—namely that the term 'visual image' suggests perfect correlation with the retinal image. The arguments put forward earlier in this chapter, however, strongly suggest that there is as high a correlation between the immediate psycho-physical events and the psycho-physical events associated with past experience of an object as there is between the retinal image of that object and the psycho-physical events which that image gives rise to. Furthermore, even though the stimulus originates from the visual receptor cells, it is, I have suggested, inaccurate to say that the response is a series of events in the visual centre only. When we see a lemon, there are occasions when we also experience the sensation of tasting and smelling it. For this, the term 'visual image' is obviously too narrow.

Nor is it sufficient to speak of a combination of sensory images, since inner speech is involved and one cannot satisfactorily contend that 'inner speech' is a matter of sensory images only however important we may regard the sensory images as part of the meanings of words.

Let us imagine an occasion on which an adult human being perceives a particular kind of thing for the first time—say a foreign

39

fruit which he has never heard of, let alone seen, before. First, it must be noted that this may not be the first occasion on which an image of that fruit appeared as a feature in the retinal images of that person's eyes. At any instant when the eyes are open there is much more in the retinal image than is *perceived*. Indeed it is nonsense to speak of any correlation between the whole retinal image and the psycho-physical events we are now concerned with. The correlation must be with part of the retinal image. In the hypothetical case we are considering, the strange fruit, let us assume, is seen on the stall of a bazaar. On an empty basket placed behind the fruit which has attracted the attention of the observer a fly has settled in such a position that from the observer's angle it must come well within the field of vision, almost in line with the outline of the fruit and not so far behind it that it is very much, if at all, out of focus. But the fly is not seen. It is part of the retinal image but it is a part which has no cortical effects, or at least none that are of the same kind as those which originate from that part of the retinal image which contains the fruit. The fly has no existence in the consciousness of the observer. And yet the general background of the fruit will be within the observer's consciousness. This fact throws some light on Rubin's 'figure-ground hypothesis' for one may suggest that the ground from which the 'figure' arises is that part of the retinal image to which conscious attention is not at that moment being given.

The unfamiliar fruit is, however, we have assumed, occupying the observer's consciousness. What then happens? Immediately a process of classification begins. Is it like an apple, a gooseberry, or a banana? In this process of classification language plays an important part. The names of things with which comparisons are made will flash through the mind. If at the same time the name of the unfamiliar fruit is heard, it will become part of the whole complicated chain of events. It is important, I think, to bear in mind the complexity of the processes that are involved in such a phrase as 'the names flash through the mind' or 'the name will become part of the whole complicated chain of events'. It is so easy for such simple, deceptively simple, statements to conceal the fact that their meaning involves events of tremendous complexity.

The second time the fruit is perceived many of the cortical events will be analogous to those which took place the first time it was perceived—otherwise one would not know that one was perceiving the same object. On the other hand the events will not be a replica of those which took place at the first seeing—otherwise one would not know that one was perceiving it for the second time. To the complete set of events in such an act of perception the term *analogue* seems fitting. The visual image is only a part of the analogue and may indeed be virtually swamped by other events that take place in other brain-centres.

In what might be called the 'shaping of analogues' language is exceedingly powerful and, largely through language, so too is past experience. We shall see later that in the perception of words past experience may so work upon the visual sense as to produce visual images of words that are not on the page.

Language and Attention.

The English exponent of philosophical psychology, Stout, long ago pointed out that it was a weakness of 'the psychology of the whole' to take far too little account of the effect of attention upon perception and, as we have seen Lashley and his co-workers were of the opinion that in his theory of 'cortical fields' Köhler paid too little attention to the influence of 'habits and set' and of the other senses on perceptual experience. This cannot be too much emphasised. To put it in ordinary terms we see not only with our eyes but with our noses, and smell not only with our noses but with our eyes. There is no single sense cut off from the others, but there is no set pattern of response; the analogue which results from any particular sensory stimulus will vary with the context in which the stimulus appears, not the external context only because part of the whole context are those parts of past experience which may be incorporated into the analogue.

I have suggested that in the shaping of analogues language is of extreme importance. I have elsewhere[1] defined language as 'the index of experience' and if this definition holds good, it would seem that only by ignoring language could the Gestalt psychologists have maintained their curious position with regard to past experience. This neglect is all the more remarkable in Wertheimer's case because he actually wrote a paper on the evolution of number-concepts among primitive peoples and how that could be done without realising that what we ordinarily call 'numbers' are in fact number-words, a special branch of language, it is not very easy to conceive.

[1]*Learning and Teaching English Grammar.* Chatto and Windus, 1956.

Of the Gestalt school, Koffka is the one who has most to say about language. What he has to say about it is to be found in the section 'Ideational Learning' in *The Growth of the Mind*. His main points are as follows:

(*a*) A considerable degree of linguistic comprehension precedes ability to speak, a fact, he says, which though not known, has received less attention that it deserves.

(*b*) About the middle of the second year of life the child becomes interested in discovering the names of things, pointing to all kinds of objects and asking 'What's that?' He is satisfied when he is told the name.

(*c*) These names are as real to the child as the objects to which they belong.

(*d*) Words learned as the name of a definite thing gradually extend their range of application.

(*e*) Different words may quite early be combined into a new word, e.g. *ei* having been learned as the name for egg and *hafa* as the name of the act of raising or taking up, *ei-hafa* is used for *egg-spoon*. (Stumpf).

Referring to the period during which the child is becoming interested in discovering the names of things, Koffka writes:

> Since we have already recognised invention as an act of configuration, it follows that naming can also be regarded as a configurative achievement—it is then quite easy to assume that a word acts like any other member in incorporating itself into the pattern of a thing; that is to say, the name becomes an attribute of the thing . . . thus, for instance, a blue dress will retain its blueness even when its colour can no longer be seen in the darkness. Yet the name is a peculiar kind of attribute in that *anything* may possess it. Thus a child can supplement anything with a name, and the name will then become the most pronounced character of the thing. In this way the ascription of a name will prepare the way for a further organisation of the thing's attributes.

Again:

> When a new thing receives an old name, we should interpret that fact by saying that the new thing enters into a configuration which was acquired with something else. The new thing does not need to be identical with this other thing, but only to possess certain characteristics which agree with the older configuration.

What we must try to investigate is the configuration of each separate instance in which a thing and a name stand together. Though we previously assumed that a name is added as an attribute of the thing, this is to be understood only as a general outline of a hypothesis to be filled in by further investigation; for as Wertheimer has indicated, the characteristic configuration of a thing may greatly vary. "So, for instance, *red* in the statement that the wall is 'red' is quite different from *red* in the statement 'blood is red'." (Quotation from G. von Wartensleben. *Die Christliche Personlichkeit als Idealbild.*) These are problems for an investigation into infantile thought and speech to which, for lack of personal experience, I can only refer.

It is clear from these quotations that in a fumbling way Koffka was aware of how important language is in perception. Here he is using the term 'configuration' with a meaning very like that which I have given to the term 'analogue'. Unfortunately he allowed the term to obstruct his thinking about the processes for which the term stood. Yet it is interesting to see how greatly the term 'configuration' has been extended in those quotations from Koffka. Originally it stood for the concept that responses are not to single stimuli but to 'constellations of stimuli'. Now it has become everything that happens in the mind in response to a particular constellation of stimuli—in short, what I have called the analogue.

There is a commendable modesty and honesty in Koffka's admission that he had little knowledge of the development of language and thought in children. It is at the same time, however, a rather damaging admission to make in a book entitled *The Growth of the Mind.*

If the processes of human perception are to be studied at all fruitfully, a great deal of attention must be paid to the development of perception in young children, and perhaps the most notable thing about the development of a child's perception is the extent to which it is influenced by language. When a child has learned to speak, and even during the period when he is not quite articulate, those parts of the retinal image to which he pays attention are selected for him by words spoken to him, more than by anything else. Movement, light, bright colours—these attract his attention, but they do not have anything approaching the influence that language has.

Not only do words so largely decide what things a child will perceive, they also have a considerable effect on the manner in which he will perceive them. This phenomenon is not limited to childhood.

The meteorologist looking at a cloudy sky, for example, sees the clouds very differently from someone ignorant of cloud-formations. The very fact, too, that words and visual experience are often in apparent conflict has an effect upon the manner in which things are perceived. For example, the child who sees a yellow, low-growing dandelion and at the same time a red, high-growing rose knows them to be different and yet besides learning names which agree with this fact of difference he also learns a word which tells him they are the same—'flowers'. Thereby his attention is drawn towards what there is about them that is the same. On the other hand the child frequently finds himself delightedly exclaiming the name of something only to be told that he should have said something else. How many parents the first time a child has seen a sheep have found themselves saying: 'That's not a doggie: it's a sheep'. Why did the child call it a doggie in the first instance? There can be no simple answer, and to say that it looked like a dog is no answer at all but a begging of the question. What it is important to note in framing any answer is that we cannot assume that what the child perceived was not a dog to him. Hundreds, if not thousands of times in the course of his brief life that child's brain will have been interpreting retinal images with which he has learned to associate the word 'dog'. These retinal images have been very varied; there will in an ordinary child's life have been retinal images of spotted dogs, patchy dogs and 'self colour' dogs, of long low dogs and dock-tailed dogs, of smooth-haired dogs and shaggy dogs, of dogs with long lean noses and dogs with noses permanently pressed against invisible glass. And, as if that were not confusion enough, any one of the menagerie will have assumed a variety of different shapes according to what the animal was doing at the time—sleeping, sitting, running, walking, jumping. The surprising thing would be if in seeing the sheep the child had not perceived something nearly identical with what he had perceived on one or other of the occasions when he had correctly uttered 'dog'. For it is not merely a matter of the great variety of retinal images; there is also the fact that not all of any one retinal image need be perceived. If a child says 'Dog' when his parents think he should say 'Sheep', they normally let him know that he has made a mistake. How does the child remedy it? At the stage we are concerned with, the child can hardly be said to look with full consciousness for a clue that will prevent a repetition of the mistake, but he is led to experiment in a trial-and-error sort of way. His first attempt to get the right answer may be very far off the mark. He may pay less attention to the retinal image of the sheep itself than to that of the background and one may find him calling a cow a sheep apparently because he has picked up the erroneous idea that 'sheep' is the sound you make when you see an animal moving about in a green field. He then finds that this will not do and so through language he is led to a finer perception of differences.

Eye-Structure.

The Gestalt psychologists paid hardly any attention to the structure of the human eye. Yet the structure of the eye is one of the factors determining that the correlation between the retinal image[1] and the analogue will not be perfect. I have defined the retinal image as that varied pattern of light which falls upon the retina. Part of that pattern will fall upon the foveal area where the light sensitive cells are incredibly numerous. It follows that a very large number of messages relating to that part of the retinal image will reach the cortex. Outside the foveal area the light-sensitive cells are more thinly distributed and therefore from any area outside the foveal area and equal in size to it the brain receives fewer messages than from the foveal area itself. If the retinae were like photographic films on which the light-sensitive chemicals are evenly distributed, it could be maintained that any lack of correlation between the retinal image and the cortical events must be due to something in the cortex itself, but this is not so. Lack of correlation begins in the retinae themselves.

The structure of the retina determines the characteristic feature of our field of vision—that there is a fairly narrow field of highly defined perception and outside this a broader field of ill-defined perception. The highly-defined field is that part of the retinal image about which many messages are reaching the brain: the ill-defined field is that about which fewer messages are being received. Suppose, however, from some other source additional messages supplemented those scanty ones from outside the foveal area, then one would expect a widening of the area of clear definition. The following groups of letters provide some confirmation of this. The letters in the first group have been chosen so as to form approximately the same 'general pattern' as those of the second:

[1]In binocular vision there are, of course, two retinal images that are slightly divergent. A synthesis of these is part of the analogue.

Cdsttlofb

Sheffield

Fix the eyes rigorously in the 'tt' of the first group, then on the 'ff' of the second group, and it will be found that there is a great difference in the clarity of the other letters in 'Sheffield' compared with the other letters in the first group. This would be expected; it can be explained by merely saying that 'Sheffield' is familiar whereas 'Cdsttlofb' is not.

This explanation will do—but only if it is realised that the word 'familiar' implies previous experience carried over to the present. In other words the messages reaching the brain from the retinal image through the retinal cells are being supplemented by other information deriving from past experience of the printed and therefore also spoken word 'Sheffield'.

I have attempted in this chapter to draw attention to certain aspects of perception that, as we shall see, are of particular importance in the teaching of reading.

Part Two

THE
EDUCATIONAL
CONTEXT

Chapter VII

GESTALT THEORY AND EDUCATION

There was something very attractive to educationists in Gestalt theory—particularly the idea of 'insight'. This idea fitted in very well with the general climate of thought among educationists in the first half of the twentieth century. Universal elementary education had not long been a feature of English national life. The 1870 Act, it must be remembered, did not make attendance at school compulsory; it merely made compulsory the provision of schools. During the period when the national system of elementary education was thus coming into being, the teachers worked under the shadow of the system called 'payment by results'. This system had been introduced into the House of Commons by Robert Lowe with the assurance that it would by either efficient or cheap. If it was not efficient, he had said, it would be cheap; if it was not cheap, it would be efficient. From 1865 to 1896 in both denominational and Board schools this system was in full operation and in modified forms it continued into the present century. Under this system the amount of state grant that any school received depended upon two things, the number of pupil-attendances and the number of examination successes. The examinations were conducted each year for each standard by Her Majesty's Inspectors or their accredited representatives. The introduction of the system had brought severe criticism from the more far-sighted educationists, in particular Matthew Arnold. The aspect of the payment by results system which concerns us here is the nature of the annual examinations, particularly for the younger children. In Standard 1, for example, the pupils were required to be able to read 'narrative monosyllables'. The reading was to be done out of the books in use in the school. The immediate result of the system was that a premium was put upon rote learning. There had been plenty of that in any case. Now it appeared to have official approval, because the examinations were conducted in such a way that the teacher had more chance of earning his full grant if he drilled the pupils so thoroughly in the set books that they could read them upside down. Against this influence more enlightened ideas could make little headway—and more enlightened ideas were in the air, as we shall see in a brief survey of the history of teaching reading.

Perhaps the most striking characteristic of the educational methods of the first half of the twentieth century has been the reaction against the drill and rote methods of the nineteenth century. In such a context the word 'insight' acquired a certain magic. Not all of those who used the term, however, fully realised that it had a double meaning. In ordinary usage it meant merely understanding what one was doing and why one was doing it. The Gestalt psychologists, in spite of Köhler's later withdrawal, had spread around the idea that insight came in a dramatic flash that had no connection with ordinary workings of logic. This secondary implication of the term fitted in very well with some other developments that had taken place during the twentieth century. During the years immediately following World War I, one of the dominating influences in the intellectual life of the Western world was that of Freud. It is doubtful if Freud himself would have agreed with the various interpretations put upon his work, but it cannot be denied that in the world of education, into which his ideas were directly brought by such educationists as Anna Freud, Susan Isaacs, and A. S. Neill, his main influence worked in two directions: (a) it emphasised the importance of the emotional as opposed to the intellectual life; (b) it suggested that discipline might lead to the stunting of the child's emotional development.

Educationists, therefore, had powerful backing for such ideas as: "Let the child learn freely and he will learn more thoroughly"; "The child has a logic of his own"; "We must fit education to the child, not the child to education"; "Follow the child's interest and the rest will come"; "The child will learn when he is ready".

Such ideas were by no means new. They are at least as old as Rousseau, but with the reaction against the nineteenth century and the support they had from Freudian and Gestalt psychology, they struck the twentieth century with new force.

In more specific ways Gestalt theory influenced teaching methods. In the teaching of arithmetic, for example, there was a period during which 'number patterns' were the vogue, an idea deriving directly from the Gestalt 'configuration'. In the teaching of reading the situation was more complicated. Some writers did assume that words were immediately perceived 'Gestalten' but, as we shall see in surveying the history of ideas about the teaching of reading, it was not a simple matter of direct influence.

Chapter VIII

TEACHING CHILDREN TO READ: A BRIEF HISTORY

Alphabetic Method.

In spite of the ideas of Comenius referred to in a quotation on the first page of this study, the universally accepted method of teaching children to read until well into the nineteenth century was the alphabetic, or spelling method. Hornbooks and battledores were the traditional teaching material in England and the first books designed for the teaching of reading were modelled upon them. During the latter part of the eighteenth and the early part of the nineteenth century alphabet books and folding cards of one kind or another were produced in quite astonishing profusion by small jobbing printers in country towns throughout England.

The theory behind the alphabetic method was simple and straight-forward. Given the fact that children had to be taught to read an alphabetically written language, it followed (so it was thought) that an isolated letter was easier to learn than two letters in combination, and a two-letter combination was easier to learn than a three-letter one. So the child began with the single letters, went on to two-letter words spelling them out, and so to sentences with words of not more than two letters each. The idea of making the sentences interesting to children did not enter into the matter at all, and there was no thought of linking the reading matter to the child's speech. How could there be? Children in their early speech do not confine themselves to two- or three-letter words. In one book published early in the nineteenth century there occurs at the two-letter word stage the sentence:

"If he is as I am, he is in".

A sentence which belongs to the speech of neither child nor adult.

What it is most pertinent to note in the present context, however, is that in learning to read by this method pupils were first learning the parts of printed words and then building the parts up into whole words. The approach, in Wertheimer's words, was 'from below' and not 'from above' or from the whole to the part.

The first critics of the method were concerned about the fact that in learning the letters by their alphabetical names, pupils were in general associating the printed form of the letters with different sounds from those the letters had in words. In his novel *The Caxtons*, published in 1849, Lord Lytton made one of the characters say:

> A more lying, roundabout, puzzle-headed delusion than that by which we confuse the clear instincts of truth in our accursed system of spelling was never concocted by the father of falsehood. For instance, take the monosyllable 'cat'. What a brazen forehead you must have when you say c, a, t spells 'cat'; that is, three sounds forming a totally opposite compound—opposite in every detail and opposite in the whole—compose a poor little monosyllable, which, if you would say but the simple truth, the child will learn to spell simply by looking at it! How can three sounds which run thus to the ear, *see eh tee*, compose 'cat'. Don't they rather compose the sounds '*seaty*'? How can a system of education flourish that begins by so monstrous a falsehood, which the sense of hearing suffices to contradict? No wonder the hornbook is the despair of mothers.

Nevertheless it worked. Shakespeare learned to read by this method; so did Plato, Aristotle and Dante.

Phonic Method.

The contradiction between letter-names and sounds must have been noticed by many people, but it does not seem to have been thought a serious matter until the second half of the nineteenth century, when in all English-speaking countries a phonic method supplemented the alphabetic method. It should be noted, however, that in a language which was regularly spelt and in which the alphabetic name of each letter was the sound it represented in a word, the alphabetic and phonic methods would be identical. The 'new' phonic system of the nineteenth century was in a sense a very old one, for it was in effect a restatement of the meaning of letters in an alphabetic system of writing. The idea behind all phonic systems of teaching reading is as old as the alphabet itself and it is unlikely that everyone who taught children to read

English before the nineteenth century rigidly followed the pure alphabetic method. Because of the very nature of the symbols whose meaning is being taught, phonics will always keep breaking into the teaching of reading. Any teacher who says a word slowly 'indicating' each letter as she says it is, however temporarily, teaching by a phonic method. It is unlikely that this first happened as late as the nineteenth century. Teaching incidents of that sort do not, however, make a system of teaching nor constitute a recognisable teaching method.

It was in the United States that the idea of teaching reading by requiring pupils to sound rather than name the letters was first put forward as a reasoned policy and it was advocated in 1782 by no less a person than the redoubtable Noah Webster, the dictionary-maker. Webster, however, advocated this policy for political, not pedagogical, reasons. He thought that this method of teaching reading would foster greater political unity by reducing differences of speech between widely separated communities. E. A. Betts in *Elementary English*, October 1956, stated that Webster revolutionised the teaching of reading in the United States by his advocacy of teaching the letter-sounds, instead of the letter-names, but it is unlikely that the alphabetic method disappeared with such suddenness as to justify the use of the word 'revolutionised' in this context.

Early 'Word-Method'.

But a different kind of reaction against the alphabetic method began as early as the 1820's in America. Nila Banton Smith quotes the following from Worcester's *Primer of the English Language* published in 1828:

> It is not, perhaps, very important that a child know the letters before he begins to read. It may learn first to read words by seeing them, hearing them pronounced, and having their meanings illustrated, and afterwards it may learn to analyse them or name the letters of which they are composed.

Anderson and Dearborn, quoting this, give Worcester the credit of being the first American ever to advocate the word method.

It is, perhaps, of some importance to note that 'knowing the letters' is a phrase often vaguely used. There is little doubt however that Worcester meant the ability to give the letters their alphabetic names on being shown the printed shapes.

Again quoting Smith, Anderson and Dearborn give the following passage from *My Little Primer* by Josiah Bumstead, published in 1840:

> In teaching reading the general practice has been to begin with the alphabet, and drill the child upon the letters, month after month, until he is supposed to have acquired them. This method, so irksome and vexatious to both teacher and scholar, is now giving place to another which experience has proved to be more philosophical, intelligent, pleasant and rapid. It is that of beginning with familiar and easy *words*, instead of *letters*.

It is to be noted here that Bumstead's word method began with *easy* words, and there can be no doubt that at that period 'easy' in this context implied shortness.

Only six years later, in 1846, there was published *John's First Book*, or *The Child's First Reader* by John Russell Webb. Of this book the *New York School Journal*, as quoted in a later edition of Webb's reading book, said: 'That book was the means of a great reform. Millions of children have been saved years of drudgery by the use of the method it proposed, and Mr. Webb is entitled to unlimited praise'.

Flesch quotes at length the preface to the 1855 edition of Webb's book, by this time known as *Webb's Normal Reader*, and the passage he quotes is an account of the origin of the word method in Webb's mind. It happened almost by chance. Before breakfast in his lodgings one morning Webb was chatting to the four or five year old child of his landlady. The child's father was milking a cow outside. Webb's eye caught the word 'cow' in the newspaper he had been reading. He pointed the word out to the child, at the same time calling her attention to the real cow that was being milked, and the child ran to her mother with the newspaper calling: "I know what it means! I know what it means! It is a cow just like what papa is milking!" Out of this simple experience, according to this later preface, Webb built up his word-system.

Successful though the Webb readers appear to have been, they did not sweep other methods out of American schools. Throughout the nineteenth century and into the twentieth, the standard books for teaching reading in America remained *The McGuffey Readers*. The reading matter on a typical page of the first-stage *McGuffey Reader* was:

Is it an ox?

It is an ox.
It is my ox.

Witty quotes an estimate of 200,000,000 single books as the number of *McGuffey Readers* sold between the 1820's and the 1920's.

It is reasonable to suppose that such readers were used as alphabetic method readers by some teachers and as phonic method readers by others. Even at the present-day in England one hears of teachers who insist on pupils 'spelling out' and not 'sounding out' the words in their reading-books.

The alphabetic method gave way to the phonic method rather more slowly in England than in America. There have been various suggestions as to who was the English inventor of 'the phonic method'. W. D. Berry, Director of Education for Wakefield, quoting reports of Her Majesty's Inspectors, has made out a case for a Wakefield school-master as the inventor of 'the phonic method' during the sixties of last century. Miss Nellie Dale of Wimbledon has also been frequently credited with this 'invention'. It can hardly be said, however, that anyone invented *the* phonic method of teaching reading any more than it can be said that any one person invented the alphabet. The most one can say is that at various times creative teachers have devised different methods of presenting the fundamentals of reading to pupils. Some of these methods have been remembered and associated with the particular teachers who devised them, and most of them during the nineteenth century were based upon the idea of sounding the letters and building up the words from the letters as sounded. That is, there were individual variations of what is, somewhat loosely, called 'the phonic method'.

Reading Without Tears.

The elaborate care with which teaching material was designed to fit in with the nineteenth century phonic method is well illustrated by the nineteenth century book *Reading Without Tears, a Pleasant Mode of Learning to Read.* This book appeared before the introduction of a phonic method into a Wakefield school and long before Nellie Dale had started teaching by her celebrated method. The copy in my possession was presented by her mother to Cecilia Crompton in November 1905. It is a new edition published in 1904 by Longman's, Green & Co. (The first edition was published in 1857 by Hatchards.)

The author is anonymous, being described only as 'Author of *Peep of Day*, etc., etc.', this being 'A series of the Earliest Religious Instruction the Infant Mind is Capable of Receiving' which was originally published in 1833 and had sold about a million copies in England besides several American editions and translations into French, German, Russian, Samoan, Chinese and 'many other languages'.

Reading Without Tears was in two parts. Part One contained 274 pages and Part Two 292. Printed on heavy paper, they make a volume of a size that seems extraordinary to us today, but which might well have appeared normal to generations as familiar with the Bible as many Victorian households were.

The preface to *Reading Without Tears* is a real period-piece and yet it contains statements which clearly indicate that many of the questions which trouble teachers today were very much present in the minds of teachers in the nineteenth century. The author, for example, states that the children are not to be forced to read but are to be *allowed* to do so.

To allow them to tread the path of knowledge, steps have been cut in the steep rock, and flowers have been planted by the wayside. Pictures are those flowers—careful arrangement and exact classification are those steps.

It is often assumed that the idea of not forcing a child to read before he is ready is a twentieth century one, but this is not so. Twentieth century educators said it was advisable to wait *longer*. That was the difference. 'Let them not begin too soon', wrote the author of *Reading Without Tears*, 'never before four, sometimes not till five'. Many twentieth century psychologists have stated that children are not ready to learn to read until they have reached a mental age of seven. 'Let no parent imagine' this anonymous author wrote, 'that by beginning *late* to learn to read, or by occasionally omitting a lesson—the future eminence of the child is hazarded . . . *Happily, children are generally too inattentive to derive injury from learning*'. [My italics].

In a notice to teachers the author points out that four means are used in the book to facilitate the child's progress—'pictures, classification, the omission of irregular words, and above all phonetic names for the consonants'. 'The usual names of the consonants' he adds, 'often mislead the learner'.

There then comes these paragraphs.

The great difficulty in learning to read our own language arises from the anomalies of its spelling. Why is the *e* in *bread* short and in *bean* long? These irregularities occasion the child continual perplexity and render it dependent upon memory alone. The reflecting child who argues from analogy will certainly fall into error, while the child possessed of a mechanical memory will be more successful. But if—of all the powers of the mind—the reasoning are the most important, the system on which reading is taught ought to be one calculated to strengthen and not to suppress them.

The actual teaching material in Part One of *Reading Without Tears* was as follows:

(*a*) Fourteen pages to teach children to recognise the letters of the alphabet both capital and small. With each letter, whether capital or small, there was a picture with a remark on the form of the letter to help to impress it on the child's memory.

(*b*) Twenty pages with further work on the isolated letters.

(*c*) A page introducing the short vowels by means of the words *apple, egg, inkstand, orange* and *umbrella*, each with its appropriate picture.

(*d*) A clear run of fifty-four pages of three-letter word practice in the short vowels.

(*e*) Forty-three pages of practice with sentences containing phonically simple words, e.g. *I had a cat, I had a mat.*

(*f*) Further sounding practice as follows:

> Ba be bi bo bu
> and
> ab eb ib ob ub

On page 118 the pupil read his first story and this is how the story began:

> Bill is a big lad.
> Bill has a cob.
> A cob is a big nag.
> Bill can get on his cob . . .

Nellie Dale.

In the *Teacher's Encyclopedia*, published in 1911, there occur these sentences:

> Miss Dale's method of teaching reading has won the appro- bation of educationists because it is a system of sense-training in the first instance. One can quite understand how it must have come as a revelation to teachers who had been grinding away at reading for reading's sake—a process well calculated to develop a distaste for the subject in both teachers and taught.

Miss Nellie Dale's method, which she developed in a school in Wimbledon in the closing years of last century, was a phonic method. Superficially it bore a close resemblance to that of *Reading Without Tears*, but in practice it was very different. Its basis was still the letters and their sounds, but a year might elapse before a child saw a printed letter, for it was one of Miss Dale's principles not to show children letters until they had had a very thorough ear, hand and eye-training. During the first months the children listened to stories, were encouraged to speak and above all, were required to pick out the sounds in words— the initial sounds, the middle sounds, and the final sounds: they were at the same time given training in the making of specific sounds and were required to draw some of the objects whose names had been associated with particular sounds. Miss Dale held the view very strongly that until children had had a good deal of practice in listening to the different sounds of which words were composed letters could mean little or nothing to them. She held further that children should know what a symbol was before they were required to learn letter- symbols and so there were in her *Further Notes on the Teaching of Reading* (1902) specific suggestions as to how to teach children about signs, beginning with such an ordinary sign as waving goodbye. The training of eye and hand came into the preliminary work through chalk and crayon drawings and embroidery cards. All throughout this preliminary work the child's interests were followed as closely as possible. What Miss Dale did therefore was to suggest a systematic course of pre-reading activity which would prepare the child to come with some understanding and interest to the learning of the symbols making up printed words.

Apart from this insistence upon sense-training, understanding and interest at the early stages, Miss Dale's system had a great deal in common with the traditional phonic system of *Reading Without Tears*.

The fact that Miss Dale's method was fairly widely accepted in English elementary schools is one of the first signs that the 'payment by results' system was slackening its hold upon English education. It was in the Code of 1890 that set standards in the three R's ceased to be part of the grant system. Had it not been for the 'payment by results' system it is highly probable that the reaction against the mechanical drill in reading would have set in much sooner, for the ideas of Froebel had attracted some public attention at an educational exhibition in London as early as 1854 and in the following year Dickens expounded Froebel's ideas to the wide reading public of *Household Words*. The Froebel Society was itself founded in 1874 and the National Froebel Union was founded as an examining body for infant teachers in 1888.

It should be noted that in proportion to the population there were far more children under five at school than there are today. The Board of Education's *Infant and Nursery Schools* gives the following figures as percentages of the total under-five age groups attending school:

1870—1	..	24.2
1880—1	..	29.3
1890—1	..	33.2
1900—1	..	43.1

Various reports, however, complain that even where there was Froebelian apparatus in the schools the teaching was of far too mechanical a character. In 1893 the Department issued a special circular to H.M. Inspectors on the Training and Teaching of Infants (Circ. No. 322 dated 6th February, 1893). In this circular two leading principles were set forth as 'a sound basis for the education of early childhood':

(1) The recognition of the child's spontaneous activity, and the stimulation of this activity in certain well-defined directions by the teacher.

(2) The harmonious and complete development of the whole of the child's faculties. The teacher should pay especial regard to the love of movement, to the observant use of the organs of sense, especially those of sight and touch and to that eager desire of questioning which intelligent children exhibit.

Freedom for the Teacher.

The long-established influence of the 'payment-by-results' system could not be cancelled out in a day, but gradually in the freer atmosphere of the twentieth century changes set in and with the changes came a greater degree of diversity in what was actually going on inside the schools. Uniformity indeed is the last thing to look for today in English schools. Cuisenaire whose system of teaching arithmetic has been universally adopted in Belgian schools, once remarked: 'In Belgium I had only to persuade the Director of Education. In England I have to persuade everybody'. And so it is with reading. There was, and is, no official policy as to how reading should be taught. Teachers gradually became free to teach as they thought fit. Indeed if there was any official policy it was of freedom for teachers.

The Ministry's report, *Language* (1954) states:

The truth is that to those who do not have to teach infant children to read, the achievement is a near miracle. Those who have to do it know that, whatever their psychological assumptions, whatever their nominal choice of 'method' they are not, in fact, either the prisoners or the beneficiaries of any set routine. They may rely broadly on one system of principles rather than another, but, like all artists and craftsmen, they perform their miracles empirically, drawing more on experience than on precept, taking their material as it comes, with all its plasticity and all its intractability, solving one problem at a time, changing their tools when necessary, and blending 'methods' to suit the circumstances and the pupils.

Though that was written as recently as 1954, it expresses the habitual view of official reports. For example, in the report *Infant and Nursery Schools* (1933) a very similar view is expressed:

In the old 'Look and Say' method the child learns to recognise words by their appearance through their repeated occurrence in simple reading matter, while the various 'phonic' methods aim at making the child independent of his teacher by giving him a method by which he can discover the pronunciation of the word for himself and analyse longer words into their phonetic elements. In the more recent 'sentence' methods the child is introduced to words in the performance of their natural function as components of a complete sentence, and learn to recognise them as part of a whole. Each of these methods emphasises important teaching elements in learning to read, and most teachers borrow something from each of them to meet the need of the moment or the special difficulties of different children.

It is interesting to note that the 'look and say' method, which is another name for the 'word method' was officially regarded as 'old' in 1933.

It is not easy to trace the various steps by which the various phonic methods were ousted from English schools, but it is probably true to say that the growing interest in 'wholeness' which we have noted as the preoccupation of von Ehrenfels and others late in the nineteenth century set a climate of thought out of which there developed not only Gestalt psychology itself but also a theoretical and apparently scientific backing for both 'word' and 'sentence' methods.

Early Experiments.

Of particular interest and significance are certain experiments into the perception of words which were carried out in Germany by both American and German psychologists. The most important of these was an investigation reported by J. McK. Cattell in 1885. He found that during a brief exposure of the order of 100 milli-seconds adult readers could perceive only three or four unrelated letters, up to about twelve letters in two unrelated words and approximately twenty-four letters when they formed connected words. This study is described as a landmark by Anderson and Dearborn in their *Psychology of Teaching Reading* who in a section headed 'Psychological Rationale of the Word Method' write, 'If the limit for unrelated letters was only three or four, the words obviously were not perceived in terms of letters, the experiment definitely proved that we do not ordinarily read by letters but by whole-word units'. Cattell's results were confirmed in 1898 by Erdmann and Dodge. According to Anderson and Dearborn these findings delivered a damaging blow to the alphabetic method—meaning no doubt both letter-based methods, alphabetic and phonic.

Anderson and Dearborn went on:

The old notion had been that words were read by compounding the letters. That this is not the case was clearly demonstrated by the finding that words can be read when there is no time to grasp all the letters. Words must, therefore, be perceived in some other way. Cattell believed that the cue for recognition was the 'total word picture', while Erdmann and Dodge used the expression 'general word shape'.

And again:

If we do not ordinarily read by spelling out the word or even by sounding it out in detail, little is gained by teaching the child his sounds and letters as a first step to reading. More rapid results are generally obtained by the direct method of simply showing the word to the child and telling him what it is.

Anderson and Dearborn were writing in the early fifties. During the fifty odd years that elapsed between the investigations referred to and this comment on them, much had been written about the teaching of reading, over 10,000 books and articles, and of these only a negligible number had suggested that pupils should learn letters before they learned to read words. There were many books, however, which suggested that pupils should be given not separate words, but whole sentences to read at the very start of their reading. Although the Ministry of Education report quoted above referred in 1933 to the 'old look-and-say' methods and 'the more recent sentence methods' it is not a simple matter to place these two methods chronologically like that, for not only do schools in England vary greatly but also these two 'methods' are sometimes not easily distinguishable. There may in fact be little effective difference between two lessons in which the word 'door' is taught (*a*) with *This is a door* on the blackboard accompanied by a picture, and (*b*) with the single word 'door' and an appropriate picture on the blackboard, or a card with 'door' on it pinned to the actual door. If in both these situations it is the word 'door' which the child is being taught to recognize without having his attention drawn to the letters, then in all three it is a matter of the child's having to look at 'door', to listen to the teacher saying 'door' and to say 'door' himself next time he is shown the word.

There are many reading books which have several pages of sentences of this sort, e.g. *This is John. This is Janet.* The sentence method proper, however, would seem to demand sentences which say more than the single words *door, John* and *Janet* do in the examples quoted, e.g. *The door is open* or *John has a ball.*

What is common to both word and sentence methods is that they are analytic as opposed to the synthetic methods that began with the letters and built them up into words. The following quotation brings the idea out very clearly:

> The first principle to be observed in teaching reading is that things are recognised by wholes . . . the question arises 'What is a whole?' or 'What is the unit of expression?' It is now quite generally conceded that we have no ideas not logically associated with others. In other words, thoughts complete in their relations,

are the materials in the mind out of which the complete relations are constructed.

It being admitted that the thought is the unit of thinking, it necessarily follows that *the sentence is the unit of expression.*

A second principle is: we acquire a knowledge of the *parts* of an object by first 'considering' it as a whole . . . repeated recognitions reveal the characteristics of the whole, so as to separate it from other things . . . The sentence, if properly taught, will in like manner be understood as a whole better than if presented in detail. The order indicated is, first the sentence, then the words, and then the letters. The sentence being first presented as a whole, the words are discovered and after that the letters composing the words.

A moderately well-informed reader might well be excused for thinking that that was written by someone intent on applying the principles of Gestalt psychology to the teaching of reading. It was, however, written in 1895 by an American educationist named Farnham and quoted by Smith in her *American Reading Instruction.* It is a curious fact that Gestalt psychology brought no *ideas* to the teaching of reading that are not present in that statement by Farnham. What we see in this brief quotation is the linking of two trains of thought. First there is the idea of the recognition of things by wholes, an idea which may have begun to acquire importance as a result of the experiments of Cattell, Erdmann, Dodge and others. Second, there is the idea that the unit of teaching should be meaningful.

Reading OFF *the Page.*

The Board of Education report *Infant and Nursery Schools* (1933) names Dewey as having exerted considerable influence upon methods of teaching in England, pointing out that his best-known educational work *The School and Society* which was published in 1899, attracted immediate attention in England and that in 1906 J. J. Finley published a collection of Dewey's essays under the title *The Child and the Curriculum* in which the main idea is 'learning by doing'. It is unlikely that any American educator between 1900 and 1920 was uninfluenced by the educational philosophy of Dewey and one surmises that Edmund Burke Huey who in 1908 published *The Psychology and Pedagogy of Reading* was in some measure influenced by Dewey at that time Professor of Education at the recently established university of Chicago. Huey's ideas seem somewhat extraordinary even to us today who have long been accustomed to the idea that it is not necessary for children to begin to learn to read by learning the letters. Huey went even further and said it might be necessary for a reader to substitute a different word now and then for a word on the printed page. Here is this startling passage:

> Even if the child substitutes words of his own for some that are on the page, provided that those express the meaning, it is an encouraging sign that the reading has been real, and recognition of details will come as it is needed. The shock that such a statement will give to many a practical teacher of reading is but an accurate measure of the hold that a false ideal has taken of us, viz., that to read is to say just what is upon the page, instead of to *think* each in his own way, the meaning that the page suggests. Inner saying there will doubtless always be, of some sort; but not a saying that is, especially in the early reading, exactly parallel to the forms upon the page. It may even be *necessary*, if the reader is to really tell what the page suggests, to tell it in words that are somewhat variant; for reading is always of the nature of translation and, to be truthful, must be free. Both the inner utterance and reading aloud are natural in the early years and are to be encouraged, but only when left thus free, to be dominated only by the purpose of getting and expressing meanings; and until the insidious thought of reading as word-pronouncing is well worked out of our heads, it is well to place the emphasis strongly where it really belongs, on reading as *thought-getting*, independently of expression.

It is unlikely that many teachers in England would have heard of Huey or his book. I quote him not as an example of the kind of writing which directly influenced teachers in England but to indicate the climate of thought that was developing in America, for it was from that country that some of the most powerful influences upon English methods of teaching reading later emanated.

The 'Centre of Interest'.

America was not the only source of new ideas, however. I have referred to the influence of Froebel. But from Belgium also there came certain ideas about how to teach reading which had very important effects upon schools in England. These were the ideas of Decroly. In *Infant and Nursery Schools* Decroly is mentioned in a footnote only, but many people today would maintain that the teaching of reading in English infant schools has been more influenced by Decroly than by any other single person.

The basis of the Decroly system was the 'centre of interest'. The pupils were given commands to execute connected with the centre of interest, e.g. *Bring me the pear* if the centre of interest was 'fruits'. They were then shown a card with *Bring me the pear* written on it. After they were able to recognise a number of such sentences, they were given simple words—the names of objects in the room which were attached as labels to the objects. Games were introduced, e.g. cutting up sentences into words and reassembling the words into sentences. Later the words were cut up into syllables and the syllables reassembled into words. Later the study of letters and their sounds in words was carried on in a very thorough manner. In this system copying sentences played an important part. The sentences were written under pictures connected with the 'observation' lessons and copied by the pupils. Games of matching sentence to picture were played. The pupils were encouraged to draw their own pictures and compose their own sentences which the teacher helped them to write.

Decroly's reason for beginning with sentences was not merely that he was insistent that the first words a child read should be meaningful but also that he considered the sentence to be the unit of meaning, and he began with sentence commands because experience had told him that these, because of their definiteness, were more readily understood by children.

It will be noted that nothing could be more in keeping with the Gestalt idea of working from the whole to the part than Decroly's system and yet Decroly's system was fully fledged some years before the publication of Wertheimer's work on the perception of movement. It was in 1901 that Decroly founded a school for abnormal children and in 1907 that he established a school for normal children in which he put into practice the principles he had evolved during the previous six years. This school in the rue de l'Ermitage in Brussels has been called 'the school for learning through living'. So both from America in the ideas of Dewey and from the Continent in the more precisely worked out ideas of Decroly there came influences which were to revolutionise the teaching of reading in English schools. The teaching of reading in the majority of infant schools in England today is basically of a Decroly character and yet there is one great difference: in the Decroly classes the pupils were not given a reading book until they could 'identify any syllable at sight as part of a known word'. That is to say the pupils had learned to read before they were given books to read. They had learned by activity responding to spoken and then written commands, by the visual analysis of sentences into words, syllables, and letters and by copying sentences.

One of the main lines in educational publishing in the twentieth century has been the production of books that are intended to do what Decroly and his teachers did with their hand-written labels and cards arising out of the centres of interest.

This development took place mainly in the twenties and thirties and it was during that period that Gestalt theory was most widely and uncritically accepted.

From the facts so far presented it is clear that whole 'word' or 'sentence' methods of teaching reading did not develop as a result of the theories of Wertheimer, Koffka and Köhler but preceded them. These methods, however, began to flourish with considerable vigour in that same climate of thought in which towards the end of last century, and in the early years of this, Gestalt psychology had its origins. They were in a sense parallel developments.

The influence of Gestalt psychology itself on methods of teaching reading would therefore appear to have been a much more a consolidating, than a revolutionary one. The effect of Gestalt thought indeed has been to give an apparently sound philosophical and psychological backing to methods which had already been in existence for some time. About the perception of words none of the doyens of the Gestalt school had anything specific to say: their experiments were concerned with illusions and geometric forms. Writers on the teaching of reading, however, began to apply the term 'Gestalt' in a number of peculiar ways. Some of them regarded the sentence as the significant whole or Gestalt in the field of reading, others regarded the word as the Gestalt—several writers use the compound term word-Gestalt. No one, however, regarded the letter as the significant Gestalt. In view of Wertheimer's definition of a Gestalt as a whole which determines the nature of the parts, there could hardly be a more thorough-going application of the Gestalt idea to the teaching of reading than Huey's as indicated in the quotation given a few pages back.

The complete thought (i.e. the sentence) is the significant whole and so dominates the parts (i.e. the words) that if a word is read that is different from the one on the page nevertheless that word is the right word if it fits in with the thought (i.e. the significant whole). Since, however, Huey's book was published four years before Wertheimer's

Berlin lecture, it cannot be said that Huey was applying Wertheimer's ideas to the teaching of reading. But it is not unreasonable to suggest that both Huey and Wertheimer in different parts of the world and in different spheres of activity were engaged in the reaction against 'atomistic' or 'brick and mortar' or 'mechanistic' methods of learning. Huey was an extremist. His views did not find much support among teachers, but when in the twenties Gestalt theorists were making their first really powerful impact upon educational thought in the United States the kind of thinking that Huey had been putting forward so many years before received considerable impetus. In *On their Own in Reading* (1948) W. S. Gray thus describes the situation:

> By 1920 such a revolt had set in against the old 'phonic' readers that emphasis on visual word perception, whether by sight or by phonetic analysis, came to be considered almost disreputable among many school authorities. This trend reached fantastic extremes in many centres during the late twenties and early thirties. Radical thought in these years held that if a child were interested at all in reading, no teaching of specific words by any method was necessary or justified. In many schools, teachers were sternly warned by their superiors against giving any special attention to the visual form of words, whether by sight or by phonetic methods, as a preparation for reading. In these schools meaning was to be considered almost the only factor in word perception, and children were expected to identify new words by 'guessing' from context. Fortunately, even in the area of the articulate and vociferous radicals, many sensible teachers were not stampeded and continued to pay some attention to word-analysis skills.

It is highly doubtful that things could have reached such a pitch without the help of Gestalt psychology. In order to make this point clear it is necessary to refer back to traditional phonic teaching. One of the great drawbacks of traditional phonic teaching is that pupils so often stuck at the point of being able to sound out the letters while remaining unable to synthesise the letters into words. There are few things more trying to the patience of the teacher than this particular failure, all the more so since the main *raison d'être* of phonics teaching has always been that the sounding out of letters is nearer to the sound of the word than the alphabetic spelling of them is. Many of these failures were due to bad teaching and particularly to a fault in teaching which did much to rob the traditional phonic method of any advantage it was supposed to have over the alphabetic method. This fault was the habit of tacking a vowel sound on to the end of each letter as it was sounded out. With some consonants (e.g. the plosives) it is difficult to make oneself heard at the back of a class-room without adding a distinct vowel sound to the consonant and saying, for example, *per* for p. Nasal and fricative sounds, however, are free from that difficulty. Yet by analogy it became a habit of teachers to sound *s* as *ser*, *f* as *fer* and so on. This is still very common in this country where one may hear *fun* 'sounded out' as *fer - u - ner* instead of *f-f-f-u-n-n-n*. That it is common in America, too, is indicated by the fact that in 1955 the *Elementary School Journal* published an article pointing out that these superfluous vowels take away much of the benefit of phonic teaching. In Bond and Tinker's *Reading Difficulties*, published in 1957, in a test on phonic knowledge the pupil is required to 'sound' f as 'fuh'!

Another disadvantage which the old phonic method was universally found to have was that, even if the pupils did not split up the words into separate letter-units with intrusive vowels, they nevertheless did seem to form the habit of peering at the words letter by letter, a practice which was not conducive to fluent reading. Many teachers, too, were of the opinion that the attention to letters which the phonic method insisted on withdrew a child's attention from the meaning which the written words were intended to convey.

Words Without Letters.

It was to be expected then that teachers and educators would look with interest and sympathy upon any theory which promised to remove these irritations from teaching. Though in England, until the last years of the 19th century, the grant regulations made it impossible for teachers to escape from letters and monosyllabic words, Huey's book, with its fantastic theory of reading being free from the printed page, was an indication of how far in less controlled circumstances theorists were prepared to go in freeing themselves from the bondage of letters in their teaching. It was the theory of the word as a Gestalt, however, which finally established in both America and England the idea that at the early stages of reading letters were not important either to the pupil or to the designer of text books.

During the twenties and thirties the habit became established in America of no longer referring to printed words as being composed of letters but as having 'configuration', 'visual pattern', 'visual characteristics', 'word elements' and so on and by the end of the twenties, according to Flesch, nearly all primers based upon phonic concepts had disappeared from American bookshops and publishers' lists. The ideas of Gates were extremely important in determining the direction in which ideas developed in this field in America. The following quotation from Gates's *The Improvement of Reading* indicates the line of thought:

> In general, the best procedure is to attempt to recognise the word as a whole. If a quick glance at the whole configuration does not lead to recognition, the next step is to try to recognise the words in terms of large components. For example, if the child fails to recognise *without* as a whole, he should look for the big features and in doing so he may discover that he knows both of the component words. If he only knows *with* but is unfamiliar with *out*, he may be able to solve it since knowing the first part gives him a very good start. He is especially likely to solve the word if it is in a helpful context. Failing to recognise any of the words he may search for small details. In the case of this word the component words cannot be broken up into syllables, but he may recognise some of the phonograms such as *wi* or *th*. He thus may work out the first word by phonetic analysis. The second word may offer difficulty but he may know the sound of *ou*. Since it has several sounds he should try one after another, and add the sound *t*. If he is unsuccessful in this he may try to combine the sounds of *o* and *u* and *t*. In this case the task is likely to be difficult unless he shifts from the long sound of *o* to the short sound. It will be noted in dealing with this word that the whole problem is easier the larger the unit the pupil can recognise.

The *Improvement of Reading* was published in 1937 but ten years earlier Gates had published in the *Journal of Educational Psychology* an article in which these ideas were adumbrated.

In 1949 D. H. Russell gave a list of seven different ways in which new or partly known words could be recognised in his book *Children Learn to Read*. They are:

(a) The general pattern of the word;
for example, the word dog might look like

(b) Special features of a word, such as a double *t* or the tail on the end of the word *monkey*.

(c) Similarity to known words—if the child knows *pail*, he may derive *mail*.

(d) Recognition of known parts in words—in compound words such as *mailman*, or seeing small words in large words, as *fast* in *faster*.

(e) The use of context clues—an intelligent guess at the words from the meaning of the rest of the sentence.

(f) The use of pictures as clues somewhat similar to meaning.

(g) Some phonetic and structural analysis of the word.

It is notable how reluctant both these writers are to refer to letters as a means of recognising words and how little importance they attach to the order of letters in words. Nearly all writers on this subject during the last few decades have shared these weaknesses.

Chapter IX

' INTELLIGENT GUESSING '

The quotations from Farnham and Huey shows that some time before Gestalt psychology was established as a school of psychology there were some educationists who were thinking in terms of even larger wholes than words—the sentence was the unit of thought according to Farnham and in Huey's opinion it was not only a commendable thing but sometimes a necessary thing for different words to be read from those which had been printed! The important thing was that the words read should fit into the whole context. Although Wertheimer dedicated his life to the proposition that there were wholes such that their intrinsic nature determined the behaviour of the parts rather than the parts determining the whole, it is hardly likely that he would have driven his *idée fixe* quite so far as to maintain that the whole sentence determined particular words. There is, of course, a certain truth in the proposition. The context in which a word appears to some extent determines the meaning it carries at that particular time, but this is very far from saying that the context in matter being read can legitimately be allowed to dictate the reading of other words than those which are there in print.

The quotation from Gates (on page 70) gives some indication of how the idea of guessing from the context was incorporated into the 'whole' psychology of reading. A further quotation from the same book shows this more clearly:

> *The, there, those* and *a* are likely to be mistaken for each other. All these words give approximately the right idea and the

distinctions among them are usually not necessary for understanding the thought as a whole . . . Similarly words related to a common situation or a general topic such as *cow, horse, pig, sheep, chicken* are likely to be mistaken for each other . . . In teaching children, the danger is that pouncing on such errors may discourage this most intelligent and rapid device for learning new words.

Guessing from the context has acquired a new importance in recent years because of the work of Dr. W. S. Gray who directs Unesco's work on reading and has therefore international influence. Dr. Gray has written much that is of value in reading. I have on an earlier page quoted his criticism of that extreme school of thought in America which advocated a policy that seemed remarkably like teaching children to read without seeing print. Unfortunately, in spite of his insistence upon the need for training children to see words accurately, Dr. Gray has not been able to shake off the powerful influences which led so many of the experts to neglect the meaning and function of letters in their theorising about the teaching of reading. I found this to be so in a discussion I had with him after I had commented somewhat critically on a draft Unesco report and it is apparent in some of his writings. For example, in *On their Own in Reading* he says that if a child reads *Mary was the cat* instead of *Mary saw the cat* a quick reference to the context will reveal that the correct reading should have been *Mary saw the cat*. The fundamental fallacy here, however, is that it is not the context which determines that 'saw' is 'saw' and not 'was' but the order of the letters.

My reason for giving the idea a chapter to itself is not the great importance so many writers attached to it but rather the fact that no one writing in this field has to my knowledge examined closely the processes that take place when an intelligent guess from the context is made. The first thing to be noticed is that no one can make an 'intelligent guess' from a context of which he is ignorant. This is to say that enough words in the sentence have to be accurately recognised before any guessing at other words can take place. I shall later be producing evidence to show that printed words cannot be accurately perceived without the perception of the letters in them and that children trained to perceive whole words characteristically see only parts of the words and then say the whole word—frequently the wrong one. The reading material can be so designed, however, that on the basis of this part-seeing the child correctly reads enough of the words to understand the general drift of the sentence. His 'intelligent guess', if he has got the idea that the sentence is about animals on a farm, might very well be, as Gates instances, 'pig' instead of the printed 'horse'. This is at a very rudimentary stage of learning to read and at this stage it is very likely that the printed form of the word 'horse' will have made so little impression upon him that he will not recognise it even as 'pig' next time he sees it! There is a more advanced type of guessing from context, however, a type in which all fluent readers indulge. The pupil, or indeed adult, who has fully mastered the mechanics of reading and has considerable practice in the skill, indulges in intelligent guessing nearly all the time he is reading. Even in silent reading he is saying the words in sub-vocal speech. So, if he is reading the sentence: *The sun was high in the sky* he may very well have said 'sky' to himself before his eye had reached it. Because of the close interaction of the speech and visual centres about which much was said in an earlier chapter, he may very well 'see' the word 'sky' without reference to the retinal image of it and quite certainly his perception of the printed word will be more rapid because of the stimulus reaching the visual centre from the speech-centres. In this sense, therefore, intelligent guessing from the context is, as Dr. Gray maintained, an aid to word-recognition. Where he and so many others are at fault is in assuming that this activity can legitimately be encouraged with children who have not yet acquired insight into the function and meaning of letters.

Chapter X

SEEING AND NOT SEEING WORDS

A considerable amount of research has been done into the processes by which words are perceived. The brief exposure techniques of Cattell have already been mentioned; similar studies are in existence using degree of illumination and not exposure-time as the variable.

Of these, the work based upon brief-exposure techniques has most influenced the development of ideas about the teaching of reading. Although Cattell is credited by Anderson and Dearborn with having provided the scientific basis of the 'word method', much more interesting work on similar lines was done by Pillsbury (1897), who exposed for brief periods words slightly mutilated and found that in most instances the mutilations were not detected. The omission of a letter was detected in only forty per cent. and a blurred letter in fourteen per cent. From his experiments Pillsbury distinguished three sorts of clues for word recognition:

(1) The form of the whole word, determined by its length, by the projections produced by the high and low letters, and by the location of the clearly seen letters.

(2) The clearly seen letters themselves which are not confined to the immediate neighbourhood of the fixation point.

(3) The context. Pillsbury sometimes supplied context by saying, just before the exposure, a word related in meaning to the mutilated

word that was about to be shown. Woodworth quotes the interesting case in which the experimenter said 'sky' and exposed 'eanth' expecting the response 'earth'. The subject, however, read 'zenith'.

Zeitler in 1900 reached the conclusion that the high, low and capital letters were the dominant clues in the rapid recognition of words—not the general word shape. Woodworth, however, does not regard his evidence as entirely convincing because the word shape is usually well-preserved in the mis-readings. He gives a few examples:

Exposed	Read
Epaminondas	Epimenides
Praeglacial	Portugal
Agoraphobie	Agraphie

When Anderson and Dearborn writing on 'the rationale of the word method' reported the experiments of Cattell, Erdmann and Dodge, they omitted a fact of some significance, 'If the limit for unrelated letters was only three or four', they wrote, 'the words obviously were not perceived in terms of letters'. Woodworth, however, points out that Cattell, Erdmann and Dodge, and Pillsbury all reported that their subjects believed they had seen all the letters at the time of the actual exposure, but forgot some of them before reading them in his report. 'Nothing is more likely', writes Woodworth, 'unless some word suggested itself at once, brute memory would not hold all the disconnected letters. But if 0 (the observer) is not mistaken in this impression, he gets for an instant perfectly adequate cues of a correctly presented word. If for an instant he sees the word clearly, as he thinks he does, he has all the cues he could desire'. One might well ask what further cues there are!

Another suggestion to account for the difference in the numbers of letters seen as between unrelated letters and letters in words was given by Schumann who suggested that a subject's attention was likely to be differently focussed when he was expecting a row of unconnected letters instead of a word. He suggested that the subject who expected mere letters would concentrate his efforts on a small region so as to make sure of a few of them, but, expecting a word, would attempt to broaden his span so as to compass the entire word. Together with some of his pupils Schumann carried out a series of experiments in which the subjects were asked to let their attention cover the whole field. One of these investigators, Wagner, working on the lines laid down by Schumann found that when series of fifteen letters were exposed for one tenth of a second to subjects who had been instructed to let the attention cover the whole field these subjects often reported that the whole of the series appeared distinct although comparatively few could be recalled immediately after the exposure.

Summarising Wagner's results Woodworth quotes the following examples:

Letter series exposed for 100 *ms.*	*Letters reported*
L n z d w r r t s c h n f t s	L z d t s c h f t s
F r g h n w l y r h p k j s m	F h n w y j m
V a r w c z h u k z e w p o t	V a w h z k p o t

He then makes the following comments:

It is certain that 0 read the first, the last, and part of the middle of each of the series of 15 letters. The letters reported were not concentrated about a single point. This objective result seems to dispose of the hypothesis that the only letters distinctly seen lie close to the fixation point, and to justify the assertion of many competent 0's, who say that letters over a wide field are seen distinctly during the exposure. If they are seen distinctly, though only for an instant, they can act as cues for the recognition of a word; and thus we reach the conclusion that the most effective cue for reading a long word consists of a large share of the letters in the word, seen with fair distinctness for an instant.

This conclusion does not mean in the least that the word is read by spelling it out; evidence previously cited is enough to exclude that supposition. What the conclusion means is that an adequate *simultaneous* view of the word is afforded, and that this clear and detailed view of the whole word is the cue for recalling the word.

There appears to be a certain inconsistency here. Does not the word 'adequate' suggest 'sufficient' rather than 'entire'? Indeed, having just read that the most effective cue for reading a long word consists of a large share of the letters seen with fair distinctness for an instant, the reader is to be excused if he thinks that this is what the writer has in mind when he mentions an 'adequate simultaneous view'. But immediately thereafter he finds that this has become a 'clear and detailed view of the entire word'—which can only mean that all the letters are perceived, though they are not necessarily thought of as letters.

Experiments Repeated.

Because the experiments with briefly exposed words seemed to leave certain important matters out of account and because the results were so loosely interpreted I carried out a number of modified experiments of a similar kind with several hundreds of adults, sometimes individually, sometimes in groups. There are three types of situation in these experiments:

(1)   The subject is told that a word is to be briefly exposed. He is asked not to *guess* what the word is but to state precisely what he sees. The word is then exposed.

(2)   He is told which word is to be exposed, and is asked to state what he sees.

(3)   He is asked to state how much of a word, say, Birmingham, he sees on a brief exposure. A mutilated form of the word is then briefly exposed, e.g.

BIPIIIICHAM

In (1) it is found that for every person there is an exposure time during which he can see no more than one or two letters with adequate clarity. The rest of the word is a blur. This is true of at least words of four letters and more. Among hundreds of adults who have been tested I have found no exception to this rule, apart from some members of lecture-audiences who were given makeshift demonstrations. And yet from these large-scale demonstrations there did come evidence similar to that which Wiegand produced in 1908. With his brief-exposure techniques Wiegand combined the element of distance and found that at a great distance a word was seen during the exposure as a mere stripe of grey. As the distance was reduced, upward and downward projections from the stripe could be distinguished and at about the same distance single letters began to make their appearance. The letters which were first so distinguished were usually at the beginning or

78

the end of the word. More letters and familiar letter-combinations emerged until the word was entirely clear. This was confirmed in many lecture-demonstrations when what was 'seen' varied greatly according to the distance from the exposed word.

In (2) it was established with equal definiteness that when it was previously known which word was to be exposed the subject then saw the whole word in that fraction of time during which in the conditions of (1) he was able to distinguish only one or two letters. This holds whether or not the same word is employed in the two different experiments.

Why should so much more be 'seen' under the conditions of (2) than under the conditions of (1)? To say that in (2) the subject already knew what he was about to see is not a satisfactory answer to the question. In what sense 'knew'? In what sense 'see'?

The results of experiments of type (3) bring us some way towards a more satisfactory explanation, however. Since, as tests (1) showed, there is an exposure time too brief for anything but a vague grey shape to be seen, it is possible to expose the mutilated word so briefly that no characteristic, mutilated or otherwise, is perceptible. On the other hand if the exposure time is increased the subject will 'see' the entire word even though it is not there in print; if the exposure time is increased still further the mutilation will, of course, be noticed.

The following deductions may be made and are, it seems, of universal application:

(1) Words are not perceived *immediately*. Whether the word to be exposed is previously known or not, if it is presented for a period of the order of one-hundredth of a second, it will be seen as a grey band.

(2) A subject who is dependent solely upon the retinal image and his own previous knowledge of the printed word in general will, as the exposure-time is gradually increased, distinguish parts of the word. That is, he does not see it in all its details either immediately or simultaneously.

(3) When a subject is led to expect to see a particular word by being told which word is to be exposed, he will 'see' that word in its entirety in that fraction of time during which without this information he is able to distinguish only a letter or two.

79

(4)   In certain definite circumstances a subject will 'see' a whole word in all its details even if all the details are not there. These circumstances are (*a*) that he should be expecting to see a particular word (*b*) that what is exposed should bear a close resemblance to what he is expecting to see (*c*) that the time of exposure should be so brief as to prevent a close examination of what has been shown.

These experiments may very easily be repeated by anyone who cares to do so. They require no more equipment than paper, pencil and a card with a slot cut in it which may be rapidly drawn across a printed word so as to expose it briefly. This is perhaps the most satisfactory type of psychological experiment. The results can be tested for accuracy on the spot and there is no need for elaborate statistical tables because the element of chance does not enter into it. There is no question of probability but of certainty. The only disadvantage the experiments have is that they are so simple and straightforward as to be nearly incredible in the field of educational psychology where belief on the part of the reader is so highly correlated with the ability on the part of the writer to blind people with science.

The chief fact which these experiments establish is that when no information reaches the brain except that which comes from the retinal image a process of visual analysis takes place. On the other hand when appropriate supplementary information reaches the brain the act of perception may be so speeded up that the whole word in complete detail appears to be seen instantaneously. The qualification has to be made, however, that this supplementary information may in certain circumstances affect the visual centre in such a way as to produce the sensation of seeing a whole word in full detail even when the full details are not all there to be seen. This is a clear example of one type of optical illusion which occurs when we attribute to the eye information which reaches in through the ear and that information is subsequently found to be false. The only difference between this type of optical illusion and ordinary acts of visual perception is that in the one case we are caught out, in the other we are not.

The condition to be fulfilled if supplementary information is to have these effects upon the visual perception of words is that the perceiving brain must have had previous visual experience of the word or must be sufficiently familiar with letters and their common sound-meanings to visualise how a word not previously seen in print is likely to appear. Neither of these conditions is fulfilled with a child at the earliest stages of learning to read.

Whole-Seeing: Child and Adult.

The statement "Children see words as wholes" has frequently been used with the implication that no visual analysis is necessary for the accurate perception of a word. Parallel with this is the statement that adults are not conscious of letters when they are reading, with the implication that there is no reason why children should be either. There is indeed a sense in which children before they learn to read do see words as wholes, as when

black cat

is perceived not as eight units of black upon white but as *two* groups of vaguely perceived and unclassified black marks upon paper. The quality of the perception here is similar to that of the adult who sees a word too briefly to be sure of anything except that it was one word not two as in a brief exposure experiment or when he flashes past a station name-board in an express train.

There is a world of difference between whole-perception of this quality and that whole perception of the adult which, the phrase goes, enables him to take in whole words and even whole phrases at a glance. Perception of this kind, as we have seen, is very far from being a matter of the eye alone and is impossible without a great deal of experience of the printed word. Writers of articles and books, however, gaily go on using the phrase 'recognising words as wholes' as not only having a precise meaning but as having the authority of a complete system of psychology behind it, indeed, as I pointed out in Chapter I, a recent book on reading published claims that this is one of the main discoveries of modern psychology.

The experiments of Cattell, Erdmann and Dodge were carried out towards the end of last century. That they were still being quoted as authoritative in the fifties is probably largely due to the fact that for so long anything in line with the theory of the 'whole' was blanketed from criticism in the woolly folds of Gestalt theory.

In the chapter outlining the development of ideas about the teaching of reading, the quotations from Gates and Russell in particular show the general trend of ideas as to how words are perceived and, since all these aspects of reading are inextricably bound up together, I have said something on this topic in the chapter on the theory of

81

intelligent guessing from the context. The quotation from Gates on page 70 is especially interesting. He recommends that the best procedure when a young reader has some doubt about a printed word is to attempt to recognise the word as a whole. 'If a quick glance at the whole configuration does not lead to recognition, the next step is to try to recognise the word in terms of large components . . .' and so on.

Here the whole printed word is regarded as the Gestalt and this Gestalt, we are told, is best recognised as a whole.

But, as we have seen, 'as a whole' is a phrase which not only allows but actually demands different interpretations in different contexts. The gross, undifferentiated whole-seeing of the very young child or of the adult in brief exposure experiments with words out of context is of no value in discriminating between one word and another for there are very few words indeed in English which perceived so grossly could not be confused with many other words. On the other hand there can be no problem of recognition if the reader is experienced enough to see the word as a whole in the second sense discussed earlier, for this kind of whole-seeing is possible only when a word is already familiar. So Gates's 'best way' of solving a problem of word-recognition is impossible—except after the problem has been solved!

It was F. J. Schonell who more than any other single writer lodged Gestalt ideas in the minds of English educationists. His *Backwardness in the Basic Subjects* first published in 1939 has for long been regarded as a classic of pedagogical literature. In this book one reads that the first obvious feature which children perceive in a word is the general shape; in the same section one reads that children frequently recognise words by specific details, e.g. the dot on an i or the tail of a y, as in *monkey*; it is also suggested that the early reading material should be so designed that words of as different shape as possible occur near one another and words of similar shape should be kept as far apart as possible, preferably in different lessons. It is suggested, too, that *The cat sat in the frying-pan*, accompanied by a humorous drawing is a more suitable sentence for a first reader than the classic *The cat sat on the mat*.

In his *Psychology and Teaching of Reading*, too, Schonell was able with the same imperturbability to assert that children were recognising whole configurations at the same time as he was reporting evidence that they depended upon particular details for successful recognition. In the opening pages of the book he is writing about Malcolm aged $4\frac{1}{2}$ who is able to discriminate between the names

MALCOLM

PAT

BARRIE

printed on cards in capital letters. Malcolm 'does not know the names of more than two or three letters nor the sounds of any letters'. Because of this limited knowledge it is according to Schonell 'obvious . . . that he is responding primarily to the total visual pattern of the whole word, and it is the marked difference in the visual patterns of the words which enables him to recognise each word . . . For example, his own name, MALCOLM, starts with M and finishes with M; this gives it a certain discriminatory characteristic apart from its length . . . and so on'. He adds that BARRIE is distinguished by the letter E—'a letter which Malcolm remembers from his attempts to write the name of his friend Peter, when he was told that E has three arms, one long one at the top, a short one at the middle and a long one at the bottom'.

E. R. Boyce in *Learning to Read* follows the Schonell line of thought quite closely but with much less self-contradiction. She states that when a child first looks at a word, he sees a set of confused markings on the paper from which details gradually emerge as, for example, the 'two little eyes peeping out of *moon*'. There is no reason to suppose that the emergence of details is not the normal way in which perception develops. Unfortunately the child who recognises 'moon' in that way is not perceiving the printed word 'moon' accurately and common sense would suggest that Schonell's suggestion of having early reading material of as differently shaped words as possible would result in encouraging the child to be satisfied with inadequate perception. There is nothing wrong with Miss Boyce's description of how the perception of a word naturally develops. It is the conclusions that are drawn that are so erroneous, as, for example, when she says 'long words are also easy provided that they convey meaning, e.g. elephant, aeroplane, rhinoceros'. 'Rhinoceros' is an easy word to read compared with words like 'bus' and 'cat' only if one is willing to say a child is reading when he picks out a word merely because it has a strikingly different shape from other words with which he has acquired some familiarity. If a child were to be shown a picture of a rhinoceros at a zoo with the caption

The rhinoceros in the Zoo

he would not have much difficulty in picking out 'rhinoceros' without bothering to look at it carefully—it is the only long word in the sentence. 'Reading it is!' exclaims Miss Boyce as she describes this kind of feat. Children who have got no nearer reading than that, however, will even without the picture gaily read 'The rhinoceros is in the Zoo' when they are shown, with a picture of a rhinoceros, such 'sentences' as

<blockquote>
The bicycle is in the Zoo

The restaurant is in the Zoo

The chinoiserie is in the Zoo

The cdlmcovxz is in the Zoo
</blockquote>

and so on. In the well-known *Janet and John* series there occurs at an early stage the sentence, *I see the aeroplane*, which the child is expected to 'read' before he has been given any information about letters. These books were designed in America when Gates was at the height of his influence. The English edition is a great favourite in England and throughout the Commonwealth. In the schools of New Zealand at least until recently they were almost universally used and I found them highly popular in the English-speaking schools of South Africa during a lecture tour of that country in 1955. It was in South Africa that I had the astonishing experience of hearing more than half a class calling out 'aeroplane' when I wrote *ocvcglomc* on the blackboard, this although they had watched me write down each letter. A few minutes previously I had heard them 'read' fluently the *Janet and John* book in which the word 'aeroplane' occurs.

It was in South Africa in the province of Transvaal where there was published earlier in that same year a pamphlet called *The Global Reading Method*. This was distributed as a series of recommendations to teachers by the Transvaal Education Department. It begins as follows:

> A child's introduction to reading must be in the form not of a letter, nor of a sound, nor of a word, but in the form of a short, easily understood and remembered sentence . . . On no account must he get the impression that 'reading' consists of looking at or knowing or saying letters or words.
> The sentence should not be written on the blackboard nor on a chart, but on a flash card which must be flashed. The child must be taught *not* to look at and say each word separately, but at one glance to see the whole sentence and to say it is as a unit. In the

old 'phonic method' word recognition is the main aim, and so sentences had to be specially constructed with words which resemble one another; 'meaning' was a secondary consideration. According to the Gestalt psychology this is quite wrong, because it is far more difficult to learn to distinguish words that have very nearly the same appearance than to distinguish words that do not resemble one another.

In discussion with a few of the members of the committee which drew up this pamphlet I learned that the main idea they had at the back of their minds was that of training children to see large printed units, the same idea as Schonell had when in *Backwardness in the Basic Subjects* he said that one of the results of packing the child's early reading material with too many words of similar structure would be that he would have to peer at letters to procure recognition. That a wide recognition span will result from the kind of perception we have here been discussing may hardly be thought possible on logical grounds. Nevertheless before we jump to that conclusion it may be well to consider some of the facts about the development of perception in young children.

M. D. Vernon in *Backwardness in Reading* (1957) rightly deplored the fact that so much of the work on word-perception was carried out on adults and pointed out that these are studies of visual perception at the highest level and that it cannot be inferred that anything of the kind takes place in the reading of beginners. The facts reported in the following chapters help in some measure to fill this gap in our information. At the same time it is as well to bear in mind the fact that what had been discovered from the study of adult perception need not have led into such unprofitable paths if the evidence had been more carefully analysed and this careful analysis was not carried out either by Professor Vernon herself or by any of the other writers referred to so far in this book. It can hardly have been lack of intellectual power which lay behind this failure but rather the climate of thought in which they were, and to a somewhat less degree are, working, a climate which made it difficult for them to shake themselves free from the prejudices of Gestalt theory.

Part Three

EVIDENCE

FROM CHILDREN

Chapter XI

CHILDREN LEARN TO SEE

No one can find fault with modern educational theory for attaching too little importance to the child's pre-reading experience. There are whole books on the subject of getting ready to read, and all general books on the subject have a section of some size devoted to it. Indeed, the impression one has of some of the heavy, 700-page books on the teaching of reading which American publishers find it economical to produce is that the first half is devoted to preparation for reading and the rest to the improvement of reading skill. Somewhere in between in some not easily detectable way learning to read has taken place. The emphasis on pre-reading experience has logically enough reduced the emphasis on learning and teaching—logically enough, because if the idea of 'reading readiness' is taken, as it so often is, to imply that the child will read when he is ready, then the obvious thing to do is to get him ready. How one gets him ready will depend greatly upon the conclusions one has reached about the nature of reading and the nature of perception. Superimposed upon these is the idea one has of the extent of a child's pre-school experience. It has been frequently said, by Dolch for example, that a child is not ready to read until he has reached a mental age of seven. Beneath the term 'reading readiness', however, lurks an uncomfortable and unacknowledged fact—namely that those who make most of 'reading readiness' really mean by it 'that degree of maturity at which one can expect a child to understand that letters mean sounds which can be made into spoken words'. Since word-whole theory insists that the child should not see letters at the early stages, it is hardly surprising that getting them ready is a slow process.

Of course children cannot read before they have achieved a certain level of development, neither could they walk or talk, but development towards letter-knowledge can hardly be helped by teaching them to be blind to letters. Unfortunately there is no argument against the final answer of those who are prepared to give 'lack of reading readiness' as the cause of retarded reading, for if a remedial teacher scores an astonishing success with a non-reader, the answer comes pat, 'She must have got him just when he was ready'. This is a hard comment on the work of many devoted remedial teachers who have no redress except by means of an extended argument which is unlikely to be listened to.

The concept of 'reading readiness' could never have achieved the status it has if the more influential experts had a deeper knowledge of a child's earliest years. One of the results of this lack of knowledge has been that, in America particularly, the actual teaching of reading has been so much delayed that many a child, instead of getting ready to read, gets bored with waiting to be taught. To read some of the American productions on this topic is to form the impression that American children in general live in a social vacuum up to their school entry age of six. In this country the situation is not nearly so bad, not only because children go to school a year earlier but also because in England teachers in general have not been subjected to quite the same pressures from above. It is indeed remarkable how the English gift of compromise sometimes shows itself in this field. I have known teachers who had committed themselves emotionally and intellectually to modern theory in general and who would argue heatedly against anything that remotely resembled traditional teaching but whose own teaching methods incorporated enough traditional ideas to save them and the children under their care from the results of their theories. Even at the higher level there is the case of Duncan who in his book *Backwardness in Reading* states that one should aim at a direct assoc- iation between the word-pattern and the meaning and goes as far as to say that the interpolation of sound may prove a hindrance and yet produces reading books very largely based upon phonics. And there is Schonell, too, himself Australian but working in England and with English co-workers, who in spite of his insistence upon differing word-shapes in early reading material produces reading-books in which less attention is paid to that principle than to the common sense idea that letters stand for sounds. In spite of all these compromises, however, it is true to say that English education has not entirely escaped from the results of under-estimating the nature and extent of the child's pre-school experience.

In this chapter and the one that follows it I give a selection of observations I have made on the development of perception and language in young children.

Recognition of Pictures.

At the age of eighteen months the little girl A could recognise pictures of dogs, babies, chairs, tables, men, women and cats, in the sense that she was able to answer, for example, "a pussy" or "a lady" when the pictures were pointed out to her and she was asked: "What is that?" These answers were given correctly in the great majority of instances no matter in what position the objects were portrayed. That is to say, a dog was seen to be a dog whether in the picture it was sitting up, begging, standing or running. Sometimes a baby in a picture was, however, said to be a man—though never a woman. A little juggling with pictures showed that this was because men had sometimes been seen in pictures as bald—like babies. On one occasion a rather badly drawn picture of a rabbit in a story book looked to adult eyes more like a dog than a rabbit. A, however, insisted that this was a cat. This picture was traced in outline without the whiskers and it was then called a 'dog'. A set of pictures was prepared showing cats, dogs and rabbits in different positions. Whiskers were put on these at random. In every case where whiskers had been sketched in, the picture was taken to be of a cat. Houses, of course, often appeared in the various picture-books. By this time A would name the picture a house whether it had doors, or windows or not, whether it had a chimney at either side or a chimney in the middle and, of course, in real life she had seen houses of different shapes.

It is clear that the child who is to learn the meaning of, say, the words *dog* and *house* will not do so by paying attention exclusively to the outline shape of either of them: a dog has a very different shape sitting down from standing up, even its head has a different shape as seen from different angles. Sometimes according to the angle it will be seen as having one ear, sometimes as two; its tail may stick out straight as in a pointer or may be between its legs. Neither is colour any help. How then does the child learn to attach particular names to things of which his visual experience is so various? The child from his very earliest days is growing up in a world of continually changing sense impressions and that these changes are far more numerous and various in relation to the sense of sight than in relation to any of the other senses, though these are various enough. The ordinary sounds of the home apart from human voices have a certain stability—the chink of tea-cups, the crackling of the fire, the opening and closing of doors are fairly consistent. At least, even the experienced adult would find it difficult to distinguish between the crackling of the fire on one day and the next. The differences are mostly differences of direction and a baby of even three months shows some success in learning the direction of sounds. On the other hand the retinal images the child must have of the very mug he drinks out of vary enormously: sometimes it has a handle, sometimes not, sometimes on the retinal image the rim appears as a straight line, sometimes an ellipse, sometimes a circle. Sometimes the retinal image of the mug is so big as to obliterate the table, the whole visible world. One of my own earliest memories—possibly the earliest—is of being held screaming in my sister's arms looking at a strawberry which swelled and swelled until it was bigger than a bookcase that occupied a whole wall in the room. For about forty years I regarded this strawberry as a terrifying hallucination and then I realised that probably at that early age I had not had enough visual experience to distinguish in size between the bookcase which I knew to be big and the strawberry which as it was brought near to my eyes gradually obliterated the image of the book-case on the retina.

There appear to be two ways in which the child imposes order upon this chaos. One is, as we have seen, the selection of details—as when, other things being more or less equal, the child regards whiskers as the distinctive feature of a cat, having *learned* that in pictures cats usually have whiskers. But the details must be sufficient: by a process of trial and error, as was suggested in an earlier chapter, the child gradually learns to regard some details as being insufficient. How quickly details may acquire or lose significance is shown by the following events all of which took place in three minutes.

A, was shown a circle and was asked what that was a picture of. She replied "A ball". It is perhaps worthy of notice that a ball is one of the comparatively few things of which the retinal image remains fairly constant apart from size no matter what the angle of vision is.

When, however, she was shown two circles and asked what that was a picture of, she made no response. Why? Was she perceiving this as a new 'whole' rather than as two separate pictures of two balls. At this time the word 'two' had recently been brought into her speaking vocabulary ('Daddy come to Mummy—now two') and she might therefore have been expected to say 'two balls' or 'one ball' and another ball. On the other hand it seems more likely that her mental 'set' was towards seeing a picture of one object. She had at the time a habit of asking me to 'draw a lady' and was therefore accustomed to see me doing a lot more than drawing two circles before the drawing of one object was complete.

The progressive responses in the next few minutes were as follows:

 No response.

 'Glasses'. (The first time she had seen these as a drawing. She had often shown a keen interest in mine, however.)

 'Bicycle'.

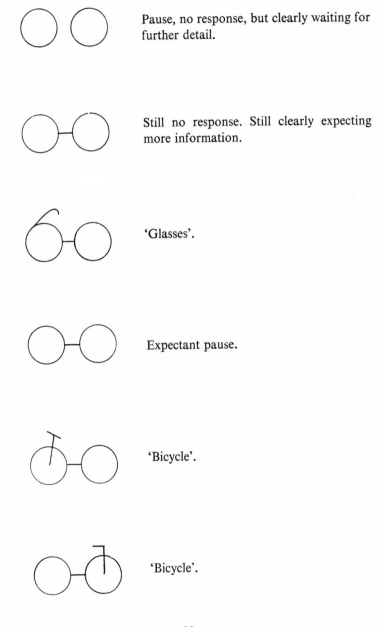

Pause, no response, but clearly waiting for further detail.

Still no response. Still clearly expecting more information.

'Glasses'.

Expectant pause.

'Bicycle'.

'Bicycle'.

A, was at this time in her twentieth month. One may well wonder why so many writers attach so much importance to the outline shape of words for children three times that age;

the outline shape of

is different from that of

and similarly

is different in outline shape from

Of course things have an outline shape. If they are perceived at all as separate things, there must be in the field of perception a boundary between the separated 'thing' and that from which it is separated, which is no doubt what Hamlyn meant in the criticism of the 'figure-ground hypothesis' quoted in Part One of this book. It is true too, that that outline shape may be said to accord with the Gestalt law of 'closure'. There is no line round a word, but we do tend to 'close' the gaps between the letters, so that *caravan* can be said to have the shape of a long rectangle and *bloom* the shape of a railway engine travelling to the left. But such outline shapes are of little value in recognition. Nor is it generally the significant detail alone which enables a child to make order out of the chaos of impressions. More important is the relationship between details. 'Whiskers' put on a dog's tail did not turn the dog into a cat, but whiskers put on a dog on the right place did. The detail is not seen in isolation from the whole.

Perception at least after the acquisition of the first words appears to be inextricably tied up with concept forming. In studying the process one becomes very much aware of the abstract nature of nouns commonly called concrete. The word 'shop' for example, was in A's vocabulary. Yet all the shops she knew were different in appearance. Some had men serving, some women, some sold newspapers and books, some sold meat and so on. Yet all these different visual impressions were subsumed under the term 'shop'. What was the common factor, or factors? Probably a combination of things in the window, a place with a counter and somebody behind it, a place where you got things for money. Part of this concept forming process is the rejection of details as insignificant—a shop has windows, but so has a house; it has a door and walls, but so has a house. Therefore these are not the things that mean 'shop'.

The extent of A's speaking vocabulary gives some indication that by the time these observations were made she had so formed a fair number of concepts of an elementary kind. In the middle of her nineteenth month she had a speaking vocabulary of sixty words— among them were aeroplane (pronounced 'plane') and window cleaner. It was not possible, however, to keep an accurate record from then on because new words were being acquired rather rapidly and often behind one's back, so to speak. Two attempts at vocabulary counting were made before the end of her second year, one by writing down all the words she had been heard to use, the other by noting as far as one possibly could every word spoken on one particular day. These lists are given on a later page. On the basis of the reasonably accurate count at the end of her nineteenth month and the two later counts I estimate that at the time of the observations given above her speaking vocabulary was in the region of 100—120 words.

The Word and the Thing.

At the age of one year ten months another short series of observations was made. The first aim of these was to acquire some further information about concept-forming in relation to perception by trying to teach the meaning of the relational terms 'same' and 'different' in connection with perceived figures. Cards were made as follows:

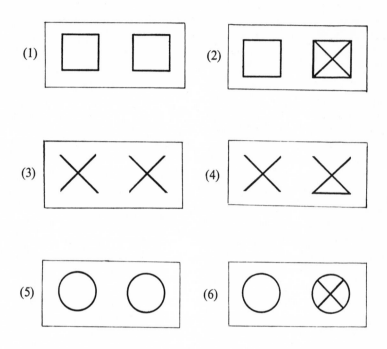

Card 1 was shown and she was told: 'Same'. Card 2 was shown and the word 'Different' was said to her. This was repeated several times. She was then given the remaining four cards and asked to pick out a 'same' one. There was a completely random response. When 'right' was substituted for 'same' and 'wrong' for 'different', and when later 'good' was substituted for 'same' and 'bad' for 'different', the response was again a completely random one. It was not expected that she would succeed in this difficult task. Yet the problem here was not one of discriminative perception so much as of linguistic comprehension. This, I think, became clear two days later. The following cards were prepared.

The square in these cards had ½in. sides and the other figures were of corresponding size. I gave her another card with a square on it, placed the six cards in front of her and asked her to give me one the same. She picked up two cards at random and handed them to me. Next I showed her one of the cards with the square on it, traced the outline with my finger, and said: 'This is a square—a square'. She echoed 'square'; I then put the cards in front of her and said: 'Now find another square'. This time she picked out the square very quickly indeed. I praised her effort, shuffled the cards and added four more as follows:

but this time she went back to random choice. It seemed as if she had lost interest. On the following morning without showing her a square again I put all the nine cards in front of her and asked her to give me the square. This time she did it with no hesitation and several times repeated this after reshuffling. There was no wrong response, and later in the day she asked to play 'the square game'. Next day I reduced the cards to half their original size and she picked out the square so easily that I decided to find out whether the same would hold with tiny figures. So I re-drew them all as small as I could with a ball-point pen. The square now had a side of 1.5 mm., and was about the size of the letter m in ordinary book type. This time she took slightly longer to find the square, but did it in two seconds or so. It was clear that 'square' was not in her mind connected with size. Yet why should it be: the retinal images of all objects vary according to the distance from the observer.

It was clear from this that the earlier failure with 'same' and 'different' had been a failure of communication rather than of visual discrimination, for not only could she see the resemblance between two squares and their difference from other figures but could also find the figure which went with the word 'square' without a matching figure to help her.

Three weeks later, being interested in the development of the perception of what are often called number-patterns, I tried to teach her to recognize the four of clubs by showing the card and saying 'This is the four of clubs'. I then put before her in succession the 4, 7, and 10, the 4, 5, and 7, the 2, 4, and 5, and the 2, 3, and 4. But when I asked for the four of clubs on each occasion the response was purely random. Thinking that perhaps it would be an easier task to distinguish between the 4 of clubs and the fours of the other suits in the pack, I placed all the fours in front of her, but again the response was a purely random one.

Two days later I showed her the four threes in the pack and asked for the three of clubs. She handed me the three of diamonds. I picked up the three of clubs, pointed to the three circles of the trefoil and said: 'This is a club, with the three round things'. She said 'Clubs with the three round things'. I then placed the cards face downwards and asked her to find the clubs. At the first attempt the first card she turned up happened to be the three of clubs and with that she was satisfied. Next time she turned up the spades first, hesitated for a moment, then she turned up the three of hearts. Immediately she turned quickly back to the spades, put her hand out apparently to give it to me, then withdrew it, and turned over the third card which was the three of clubs. Immediately and with great pleasure she exclaimed 'Three of clubs!' This she repeated several times, enjoying the game, and making no mistakes.

During the next three days I taught her to recognise diamonds equally as well as she did clubs. On the fourth day I drew in pencil *outline* a diamond, heart, club and spade. When asked for the diamonds, she picked up the spade. When the outlines were shaded in, all in black pencil, however, she identified both the diamond and the club.

The most notable thing here is how quickly the child rejects even striking characteristics of the thing perceived and yet at the same time refuses to reject other characteristics. A, had been taught that a diamond was of a particular filled in shape and *red*. She rejected the black outline shape and yet accepted the black filled in shape.

It is also of some significance in the general argument of this study that it was only after she had had certain characteristics of the square, the club, and the diamond pointed out to her and she had repeated the appropriate words that A, showed by her responses that she had learned to recognise these things. Whether the actual repeating of the words was significant or not one cannot dogmatically say, but

98

this certainly appeared to help, possibly in riveting the child's attention but possibly also because it was *active* participation on her part. H, a boy, at a similar age did far less repetition of the words spoken to him but carried out the actions nevertheless.

The First Printed Words.

At one year eleven months A had her attention drawn to printed words for the first time—three words being chosen, her name and 'Mummy' and 'Daddy'. She was shown these words separately and was told what they were. She appeared to be unable to discriminate between them, however, and no attempt was made to draw her attention to details. A week later, however, when she was out for a walk, she pointed to a metal sign which had the letters HYD on it and said her name. Her own name begins with A. Later when given cards to play with there was some indication that she had confused the H with the first letter of her own name.

At two years she was shown a card with 'bus' on it and was told "This is a bus" and a card with 'cat' on it and was told "This is a cat". When she was asked to pick out 'bus' from eight cards each with three letters on it the choice was wholly random.

Two days later the letters b, u and s were shown separately and named. She was then able to pick out the b but failed to distinguish between the other two.

Five days later she was given eight cards, four with 'bus' and four with 'cat'. She was then given one card with 'bus' on it and was asked to find another 'bus' just as she had some weeks earlier done with the square. But here, too, there was merely random selection.

Next day the letters b, u and s were again pointed out and named separately and again the 'bus' and 'cat' cards were shown and she was asked to find 'bus'. This she did correctly several times.

The following day she was given cards *bus, but, bat, bun,* and asked to find *bus*. Selection was random. She was given cards *bus, but, cat, can, cos, cus*. The game of finding *bus* from among these was played ten times: *bus* was chosen six times, *but* four times.

The theory that children go largely by the general shape of the word appears to fit the response to the second group of words, but it does not agree well with A's random responses to the first group, because if she had been going by the general shape of the word she would not have picked *but* or *bat* at all or would have picked them much less often than the others. In fact, however, in the twenty times we played this game A made the following choices: but—six times; bus—six times; bat—five times; bun—three times. What would explain both sets of responses, however, was that she was going by the letter b alone. There was still, of course, the possibility that she was incapable of seeing the differences in general shape between three-letter words. After all it seemed clear that when Schonell was writing about these matters he was thinking of quite gross differences in outline shape between words. From what I have seen of A's discriminative power I felt I could take it for granted that A, could readily pick out *bus* from a group of words as different in structure as possible. Yet others who had not seen her ready interest in these games or watched her respond would not take it for granted. I therefore prepared the following cards: *bus, aeroplane, butterfly, I, apple.* There was no wrong response when she was asked to find the 'bus' card. It would have been surprising had there been in a child who several weeks earlier had picked out a tiny square from a number of geometrical figures. Games of this sort were frequently interrupted by such requests as 'Draw a lady' or 'Draw a man'. In response to one such request at this time I drew a man and wrote under it the word 'man'. Out of this there grew the 'bus' and 'man' game of which the object was to find the 'bus' card or the 'man' card when asked. After a week of intermittent play of this sort she became highly proficient at this game. In the early stages I indulged in a practice which, although I did not know it at the time, seemed later to have a curious significance. I occasionally wrote the new word 'man' while she watched and said the word at the moment of finishing writing it. At the end of the week it seemed that here was a situation in which a child of two plus a few days knew two words 'as wholes' very well indeed. True, she had seen me writing one of the words several times so that that word had occasionally been presented to her visually piece-meal. Yet that had happened only six or seven times compared with the forty or so times both words had been shown to her as wholes. During that week no other words were shown to her because it had occurred to me that it would be interesting to see what she did when the word 'bun' was shown to her at a time when she appeared thoroughly familiar with both 'bus' and 'man'—the word 'bun' being chosen because it had elements of both the known words in it. I expected little from this beyond corroboration of the theory that she was depending on either the letter b (with possibly the help of u) or the general shape of the word, for I fully expected her to answer 'bus'. This would still leave the question unsolved as to whether the predominating factor was the general shape or the letter b. To my great surprise, however, when I placed the word 'bun' in front of her and asked what that was, she replied 'man'. This was astonishing enough, but no more astonishing than her reply when I said, "No it isn't man!" for then she placed a tiny finger on the letter n in 'bun' and said, "It *is* man!" The explanation of this is probably that during the few times on which she had watched me write the word I had said 'man' at the moment when she was paying attention to the letter which had last appeared under the point of my pencil. In these circumstances at least, therefore, the outline shape, the projecting letter and the letter b which she had previously learned to recognize were of less significance than a single letter to which her attention had apparently been quite accidentally drawn.

It was this little incident which led me to formulate for my own guidance what I have come to regard as the golden rule of research of this kind: Never assume that any response implies more than the minimum of knowledge required to produce it. I had by this time acquired enough information both from the literature on the subject and from personal observation to be quite sure than when she first saw the word 'man' A could not possibly be seeing it in the same detail as an adult does. By the time this incident occurred, however, she had seen the word so very often that I had begun to assume that she must be *seeing* the word as accurately as I was even though, since she did not know what letters meant, she could not see it with the same amount of information in the background. I had not at that time acquired more than the sketchiest fore-shadow of the ideas I have set out on the theory of the 'analogue'. It is implicit in that theory that 'information', in other words, past experience, cannot be regarded as wholly in the background during an act of conscious perception but that on the contrary selected past experiences are incorporated in such an act. This incident made one wonder how long a child might continue to be content with imperfect perception of a printed word and later observations with school children indicated that the answer was, in blunt terms: As long as he can get away with it. This does not, of course, imply some sort of original sin; it is a universal phenomenon. We do not look at every leaf in a tree in order to decide what kind of a tree it is. Nor even if we are buying a house do we look at every brick in it. In such complicated structures it is not possible for the human brain to perceive every detail let alone relate each one to all the others. Is

101

there any satisfactory response to the argument that in designing reading material on the principal of difference of general shape the child is being encouraged to continue with imperfect perception of the kind shown by A?

Influence of Training.

In order to find out something about how fuller perception of words might be achieved I made some observations on a three-year-old child B whose previous experience of print had been no more than one might expect in a child of a moderately literate family. She had a number of picture-books and had had bed-time stories read to her but had not had her attention drawn either to particular words or to letters. A at the age of two had shown that she could pick out *bus* from a number of very different looking words. But she had more experience through specific games than was usual. B was shown *bus* without a picture and told that that was 'the bus one'. Then she was shown *caravan* and told that that was 'the caravan one'. This was repeated three times. She was then asked to give me 'the caravan one'. This she did with no hesitation. A card marked *van* was added to these two, but nothing was said about it. She again had no difficulty in selecting *caravan*. Further cards were added, each additional card more closely resembling caravan in the following steps: *car, cart, carat, carve, caramel, varacan, racavan, naracav*. The number of cards placed in front of the child was not allowed to exceed six. That is to say, when *carve* was added, *bus* was withdrawn, when *caramel* was added *van* was withdrawn, and so on. As the cards were hand-written in script the card bearing caravan was changed three times in case B had come to depend upon some irrelevant peculiarity. The following outline briefly indicates what happened:

Word added	*Response*
car	Correct response very little hesitation.
cart	do.
carat	do.
carve	Correct response with rather more hesitation.
caramel	'Carve' hesitantly chosen, then rejected in favour of correct response.
varacan	Out of 6 attempts correct response occurred 4 times. The last response was, however, a wrong one indicating that the responses were random.

102

At this point for the first time some instruction was given by pointing out the difference between *varacan* and *caravan*. In the next set of six attempts there were as before four correct responses and two wrong ones, the wrong answers being, as before, *varacan* selected twice. There was no definite indication that B had learned anything from my description of the difference between the two groups of letters, unless the fact that the last three attempts were correct had any significance.

The card marked *racavan* was added and the one marked *cart* withdrawn. In the next six responses three were correct and three wrong. The card marked *varacan* was not chosen at all.

The card marked *naracan* was added and the one marked *carat* withdrawn. All six responses were correct. This surprised me and I turned to the guiding question. What is the minimum information a child must have acquired in the circumstances of these tests in order to pick out the word *caravan* correctly from the words or letter-groups

caravan, carve, caramel, varacan, racavan, naracan?

The answer appeared to be that she must at least know that it was not the short one, *carve*, that it had not a bit sticking up at one side like *caramel* and that at one end there was a mark like this C with the curved part to the outside.

I did not at that particular time test whether B had acquired anything more than that minimum information. The observation of children so young cannot run according to a rigid time-table. There followed a fortnight during which I did not see B. By the time I saw her again I had made some other cards for her to play with. There were twelve different cards, each one in duplicate, making twenty-four cards altogether. The game, which B and I played together was to put the cards into the right pairs. This is what was on the cards:

103

carat

carve   **caramel**

caravan

varacan   **cavanar**

ravacan

We played the game of sorting the cards into pairs many times. To begin with I gave B no indication as to when she was right and when wrong in her pairing of the words. She made several errors but not once did she confuse *caravan* with any other card except the one marked *cavanar* and this occurred often enough for me to be fairly certain that there were times at least when having satisfied herself that there was no sticking up bit as in *caramel* and that the set of markings long enough, she went no further than making sure that c appeared at one end of it.

The first three pictures presented no detectable difficulty, but the two with the wheelbarrow did. When I pointed out that in one the man was pulling the wheelbarrow and that in the other he was pushing it, this difficulty was completely overcome. In pairing these cards B often said 'pushing' and 'pulling' to herself—not perhaps an indication that her language was enabling her to see more clearly but almost certainly an indication that it was helping her to classify perceptions. Some may agree with me that the classifying of perceptions is an integral part of the process of perceiving.

On two occasions B picked up *caramel* and put it with *carat*. When she came to look for a card to match with the other caramel card, however, she could not find one and went back and broke up the wrong pairing. When I asked her why she did that she pointed to the letter m and, indicating 'carat', said: "This one hasn't got a bit like that".

So far I had given B very little indication as to whether she was right or wrong in her matching of the cards, but now I began to draw her attention to differences between the cards more likely to be confused. This I did not so much by direct instruction as by making deliberate mistakes myself and allowing her to discover the mistakes. Before she was bored with these cards, I was able to note that during the last nine times when she paired up the cards she confused *caravan* and *cavanar* only once—although there were two occasions when, as happened with *carat* and *caramel* earlier she went back and corrected what would otherwise have meant two wrong pairings.

I must emphasise that I was not teaching B to read. At the end of the series of games, so far as she had learned anything from me, she did not know that she had been looking at letters. It was a matter of practice in visual discrimination solely. I was interested to see how quickly a young child could learn to distinguish between quite complicated patterns which had a high degree of similarity and since my idea of what to expect had been largely based upon what I had read in books on reading, I was surprised that B had acquired in odd periods of play spread over six weeks a higher degree of skill in visual discrimination than was assumed of children two or three years older. It had been very obvious that it was the kind of material I presented to her that had directed her attention towards specific differences in the cards she had to match. I became more convinced than ever of the flaws in the theory that children should be encouraged to think they are reading when they are achieving a certain false success by discriminating between words deliberately chosen because of their gross differences in print.

One of the things said by Schonell and many others is that children find it difficult—too difficult—to discriminate between words of similar length even when the words are short. I have already referred to Schonell's statement that if one packs the child's reading vocabulary with too many words of similar structure he will have to peer at the letters to discriminate accurately between them and this will impede fluency. Now I had proved the obvious to my satisfaction—that it is more difficult to distinguish between *caravan* and *navacar* than between *car* and *caravan*. But how difficult was it for a child to distinguish between a number of three-letter words?

When A was just over three years of age, I had a copy of the proofs of Book One of the *Royal Road Readers*. On the first pages of this book there are eighteen three-letter words with matching cards. These words are: *cat, man, pig, hat, jam, nib, bat, van, ink, cup, dog, net, log, bus, fox, bed, rod, web*. With two of these words, *bus* and *man*, A was already familiar. In eleven minutes she managed to match the remaining sixteen words correctly. This could not be regarded as a typical result, however, because of A's previous experiences. Therefore I had the same play-way task set to the boy C aged two and a half. In ninety minutes of play spread over nine days C was able to match the eighteen words correctly.

In all these little experiments I had carefully excluded any reference

105

to letters as such as I was interested in examining the theory of whole-word recognition. I knew, however, that many parents teach children to recognise letters from an alphabet book at a very early age. This goes on to a much greater extent than research workers in this field normally take account of. Out of thirty children about whom I inquired no fewer than twenty-eight had at one time or another had an alphabet book and most of them had had more than one—one had had six and several had had more than three. The manager of the book department in a Nottingham shop told me from his records that in one year he had sold about as many alphabet books as there were children of one age-group in the city and his department was only one of many shops stocking this kind of book. A large number of these books are undoubtedly torn up with delight by the children on the very day they get them, but it is likely that many mothers spend some time with their children trying to teach them the letters.

Recognition of Letters.

The fact that so many experts seemed determined to keep children away from letters as long as possible made me all the more interested in discovering what the particular difficulty was in teaching young children to recognise letters. When A was two years three months I gave her a pack of Lexicon cards to play with. I choose these because the letters were in capitals. Her earlier play had been with lower-case letters. For ten days, ten to fifteen minutes at a time, we played with the cards, mostly trying to build castles with them. Occasionally I tried to point out two cards the same but she showed no interest whatsoever. When I held out one card and asked her to give me a card the same as it she either showed no interest or picked up any card at random. This happened even though I tried to focus her attention on the letters on the cards by saying: "This is ay! This is bee!" with a limited number of letters. This was one occasion on which the giving of a name had no apparent effect upon perception, and was notably different from the interest she had shown when the marks on paper, whole words to me, were given names that meant something to her. On the eleventh day of our play with the Lexicon cards I picked up J and said: "This is the jelly one!" A was very fond of table jellies. The effect was almost magical. She repeated "The jelly one" picked up the card I had pointed to and then picked up another J exclaiming "Another jelly one". There followed the 'apple one', the 'bottle one' and so on and in five minutes

106

the situation was completely transformed. A could now recognise eight of the letters under their new designations and was eager to learn more. Two days later we were playing an improvised form of patience which required the matching of all the letters of the alphabet.

I adopted a similar procedure with a boy D, two years and four months old, who had no experience at all of the kind I have reported in describing A's responses to various situations. One of D's chief interests in life at the time was a wooden hammer with which he had spent hours hammering pegs into holes and match-sticks into a lawn. Although he had none of the planned experiences of A he had developed sufficiently to be able to recognise a few objects in picture form, but he persisted in seeing hammers in the most unlikely places. A spade was legitimately called a hammer—legitimately because he pointed quite definitely to the top of the handle with its crosspiece, and that part of the drawing was as like a hammer as one could wish for. In a comic which had been handed to him so that he could amuse himself by tearing it up he found another picture of a hammer. This time it was the head-dress of a Red Indian brave which had jumped off the wearer's head when he was startled. The single feather sticking up in the centre of the head-band was the handle of the hammer, the head-band itself was the head—and all very recognisably a hammer. D, like A, was very fond of table jellies, but when he was shown J and told 'This is the jelly one' he was not listening, he was too busy pointing and exclaiming "Hammer!"—again the cross-piece joined to another straight line. When he was told, "No, not hammer—it is the jelly one" and then shown the letter T he saw the difference between the two and from then on T was 'the hammer one' and J was 'the jelly-hammer one'! In this way D learned to recognise the letters A, B, C, D, J, O, P, T and Z in five or six minutes. It could hardly be said that any teaching was done. D accepted it as a fact that A was the apple one, B the ball one, and so on. I had expected some confusion between B, D and P but there was none; I had also expected some confusion between C and O and on the second day there was, but not on the first.

From a rather bulky store of similar observations about children looking at words and letters I select two further incidents.

At the age of three and a half the little girl E was given by her parents the first book of the *McKee* readers which had not long previously been published in an English edition.

In this book the reading matter on the first page consists of the one word 'Tip', the name of a dog whose picture occupies the rest of the page. The reading matter on the second page is 'Tip, Tip' and a little girl is shown calling to the dog. After a few days this child could pick out the word 'Tip' on any page of the book on which it occurred, and since the book was designed according to the principle of few words frequently repeated, that was often. The child's parents were intelligent people and I discussed some of the principles of word-perception with them asking them to let me know if anything occurred which seemed likely to throw some light upon how the child was recognizing 'Tip'. Within the next two days the following incidents occurred. The child pointed to 'The' in a newspaper headline and exclaimed 'Tip'—in spite of the lack of the dotted i and the downward projecting p. The next day she pointed to a tin on a shelf and said "That's not Tip!" A little questioning revealed that she was referring to an inverted L, the tin being a tin of IDEAL MILK which had been placed upside down on the shelf in such a way that only the word IDEAL was visible, which meant that the inverted L was on the left side of the word. It is, of course, possible that the greater length of the word played its part, but it is at least equally possible that the child was noticing that the inverted L was like T and yet different and that what she meant was 'You'd think that was Tip, but it isn't'.

F, a child of four, was given hand-made copies of the first exercises in the *Royal Road Readers*, Book I. This consists of a series of matching exercises matching word to word. This child refused to match 'pig' to 'pig' even though she succeeded quite well with the other seventeen words in that series of tests. Questions eventually revealed that in the matching card for 'pig' the curve of the p at its lower end did not quite reach the down-stroke. There is nothing in these observations which conflicts with what others have found. Gates and Boeker in a study of word-perception among pre-school children found that it was common for children to rely on a single detail when recognising a word. Schonell quoted this evidence, inaccurately attributing it to another research-worker named Meek, and also gave some examples of his own.

What the observations I have reported do most clearly show, however, is how readily young children can be taught to see and this is an aspect of the perception of words which received very little attention from those who assumed that Gestalt psychology had shown the predominance of 'general shape' or 'configuration' in the recognition of words. In *Backwardness in Reading* Schonell refers to the frequency of errors 'due to confusion of general shape' in children's reading, but does not consider the possibility that one of the ways of producing children who will make errors due to general shape is to teach them to rely on general shape by giving them reading material constructed on his principle of selecting words of as different structure as possible. It is in fact very difficult, as we shall see, to be certain when an error is due to confusion of general shape or not. Gates, Schonell and many others who have written about the child's perception of words have drawn their evidence from children who have had whole words put before them and who have not been taught either to see, sound out, or to name the letters in the words. Indeed we have Schonell's own statement that the reading material should be designed so that the pupils would not have to peer at the letters. The pupils who saw *aeroplane* in *ocvcglomc* were quality products of the practical application of this principle. For a group of six and a half year olds to mistake *ocvcglomc* for *aeroplane* implies a high degree of training in letter-blindness. This sounds almost flippantly cynical. Yet when one thinks of it alongside the ease with which two and three year olds learn to discriminate between fairly similar words and between letters and when one notes the attention children pay to small details, it sounds more like the simple truth. By taking that muddle of thought called Gestalt psychology and mixing it with some more muddled thinking about the process of reading the experts had managed to work themselves round to the position that you could perceive words not only without perceiving but also without ever having perceived letters. They went further and said that looking at letters was a bad thing as we saw in the official Transvaal pamphlet and in Schonell's pejorative use of the word 'peer' with reference to looking at letters. Naturally it was impossible for any expert to drive this argument to its full logical conclusion and ignore the existence of letters entirely. The insistence upon not seeing the letters was confined to the early stages during which pupils by means of a considerable amount of whole-word flash card drill were expected to have learned to recognise a few score of words without having seen the letters in them. It was only after such a period that letters and their sound-values were taught and, according to the theory, only as the need arose. That is to say, when a pupil did not recognise the word 'as a whole' then he would be given a clue by having a letter or letters pointed out and/or sounded out. There was the great difficulty, too, that the education of the child had to be seen 'as a whole' and part of that education was learning to write. No expert in England or America to my knowledge succeeded in convincing himself or anyone else that a child should begin to learn to write by trying to draw the general impression he has of particular words and then work down to letters. This may be a process that goes on in a vague sort of way in some of a child's pre-school scribbling, and I believe it was seriously tried out as a method of teaching children to write by a strongly Gestalt-minded educationist in Germany, but fortunately it has generally been felt that whatever may be taught about letters in reading they are a prime necessity in writing. The admitted necessity for teaching children to recognise and write letters in order that they may be able to write words has saved even the schools of South Africa from the full effects of the theories thrust at them.

Chapter XII

CHILDREN'S VOCABULARIES AND READING BOOKS

The compilers of nineteenth century phonic reading books had no doubt about what they were doing. They were first of all providing children with a knowledge of letters and then giving the young learners words of such a kind that by applying this knowledge they would be able to say the words. It is a fully justified criticism of many of these books that they often produced sentences with little meaning and even less connection with the language of the child in ordinary life. One met such sentences, for example, as *Bob put the pot on the hot hob.* Many modern writers have poked fun at the naiveté of such books without realising that there was an equally vulnerable naiveté behind their own criticisms. Whatever faults the authors of these books had, they certainly did not fall into the error of regarding letters and the knowledge of them as a hindrance at any stage of learning to read.

The word-whole idea appeared to release the reading-book compilers from the limitations of the strictly phonic vocabulary at the early stages. After all, if it was true, as we have seen E. R. Boyce stating, that words like *aeroplane* and *rhinoceros* are easy to read provided they convey meaning, then there was no reason why any word which had meaning for a child should not appear in the first reading books. The only question was which words should be chosen.

Many of the word-whole reading-books carry on their inside cover a note testifying to the fact that the words in the book are among the commonest words in the Thorndike word-list. This word-list is contained in *The Teacher's Word Book*, a remarkable production. Thirty thousand words are listed with key-numbers indicating their frequency in written English. In order to discover this order of frequency several millions of words were counted in a considerable variety of printed material all carefully selected on a sampling basis. As if this Herculean labour were not enough, a few years later the same colossal task was done again and a new edition of the old list brought out by a new editor. This is one of the more striking examples of wasted effort in educational research. It is a very elastic imagination which can see some point in discovering how much more frequently in ordinary written English *cabbage* occurs than *parsley*. It would never have been thought profitable to carry out such a laborious task if letters had still been thought of as the essential units in teaching reading, but in any case the first few hundred words suitable for early reading books constructed on the word-whole principle are fairly obvious. They are the words one hears children using in their speech. Studies of the speech of school children have been carried out notably by the Scottish Council and by Burroughs at the University of Birmingham Institute of Education. The study of the very earliest achievements in speech is very much more difficult, however. For one thing it is very difficult sometimes to say when a sound becomes a word; for another, many sounds the child makes may be completely comprehensible words to the child and his mother but mere sounds to anyone else. As a background to the understanding of the problem of reading the study of such a book as M. M. Lewis's *Infant Speech* is indispensable. A less academic version of that book is *How Children Learn to Speak*.

Since they concentrated so much on the visual sense and particularly its maturer manifestations, the Gestalt psychologists and those influenced by them paid negligible attention to the development of speech. I have suggested that there is a continual interaction between the senses—and, in the context of reading, particularly between the senses of sight and hearing.

So far as one can judge, the child does not hear words in the same way as adults do any more than at a later stage he sees words with adult precision. It is true, of course, that there is a certain indirectness about the evidence because we cannot tell what a child hears except by inference, for there is the complicating factor that he not only has to learn to hear but also to speak. We cannot say that the child who calls chocolate 'chockle' has heard 'chockle' when the word was said to him, nor can we be certain even that he heard 'chockle' as we hear it when he made the sound himself. On the other hand there is no justification for assuming that the child's failure to reproduce sounds accurately is a matter of lack of skill in the speech muscles and their controlling nerves only. The fact that a sound is of sufficient intensity

to set the cochlea receptors vibrating does not mean that the sound is *heard*. (The ticking of a clock in a room may be loud enough to produce those vibrations, but it may be heard only sporadically or when it is consciously attended to). Further, the fact that a sound is heard does not mean that it is accurately classified. There is no more reason why a child should hear whole words accurately at the first instance than there is that he should see whole words accurately. In both cases, as indeed in the acquisition of all knowledge, a process of classification must be going on. Things are either the same or different, or partly the same and partly different. The adult who hears rapid speech in a foreign language is constantly seeking for familiar combinations of sounds which he can link to his previous experience, and, whether he is searching for meaning or not, he finds himself unable to listen to every sound, and therefore unable to hear all of them because while his attention is engaged with the classification of one vaguely familiar sound or set of sounds other sounds pass him by unclassified. A similar process to this may be assumed to be happening in the child's earliest years. Particular sounds gain significance as they impinge not so much upon the child's ears as upon his primitive emotional states. His mother's voice, because it becomes associated with food and comfort, is among the earliest to be distinguished from sounds of a similar intensity—though loud sounds will always thrust themselves upon his attention; similarly the quiet turning of a door handle which he has learned to associate with the arrival of a familiar face will draw his attention more than even the somewhat louder sound of a passing car. So the process of separating and classifying sounds goes on. From these rudimentary beginnings the child gradually develops such skill in the classification of sounds that he becomes able to attach different meanings to the same basic sounds uttered in different tones and by different voices and not only to disentangle the complicated sound-patterns of speech but also to reproduce them.

Learning to reproduce these sounds is in itself an extraordinarily complicated process, for, as we have seen earlier, it involves the hearing centre which must not only record the sound coming from outside but also check the sound the infant himself makes; it involves the speech-muscles and the kinaesthetic sense. Furthermore, in the learning of meaningful sounds this complicated process is integrated into other complicated processes—for example, the visual process when the child is learning the name of something perceived.

Order of Sounds.

One difference between hearing and sight is of some importance in the context of reading. The child has no choice as to the order in which the sounds of a word will impinge upon his ears but he has a certain freedom of choice as to the order in which he will perceive the different parts of an object. Take the spoken word *elephant*, for example, it is quite certain that whatever happens in the child's brain, the syllable *el* impinged upon his ear-drum before the sound represented by *t* did. The same cannot be said of the retinal image of a real elephant or a drawing of one. If the real elephant is far enough away, the image of it will be present as an immediate whole on the retina. If the animal indeed is far enough away, that retinal image may be completely contained in the foveal area. But the retinal image is not identical with the retinal stimulus. One child at one moment may *perceive* first the tusks and then the trunk within the configuration of the whole. The attention of another child may be first concentrated on the animal's enormous feet and then on the tusks and trunk. To a large extent the direction of his attention will be determined by his past experience. Past experience will also to some extent determine which part of a spoken word the child will pay most attention to as indicated by his attempt to say the word, but the factor of time comes into it as well. For example, it is exceedingly common for a child's first attempts to say *aeroplane* to be 'pane'. Two reasonable explanations of this are:

(1) Before the child's attention had been adequately fixed the first part of the word had already been spoken, so that he *heard* only the last syllable;

(2) In listening to the last syllable he forgot the first two. This is to say, what he *hears* is largely determined by the order in which the sounds reach him.

One can say in fact that though in early life children have whole words spoken to them, they do not hear whole words in anything like the way adults do. Before they can do so a vast experience of the classification of sounds is necessary. It is not the classification of words but of the sounds in words. That is to say, just as later the child will be visually analysing printed words, so at an earlier stage he is making an aural analysis of the sounds of words. I do not mean, of course, a conscious logical analysis. It is a process that takes place in the twilight of consciousness which can be seen taking place when the child says *ba* for *bath*, *bykesil* for *bicycle* and *gogi* for *doggie*. In this process his mother consciously helps him a great deal normally by saying words slowly or repeating them part by part. So by the time the child reaches school little trace of the fact that the process took place remains, so little indeed that the experts on reading have been content to write as though the child had been hearing whole words almost from birth whereas in fact most of the spoken sounds that reached him did not, one might say, get past his ear-drums. He had to learn not only to classify the sounds in themselves but to detect their order, both when others spoke them, or he himself was trying to reproduce them.

During the second year of life the normal infant becomes so expert in reproducing sounds that it is very difficult to keep track of the development of a child's vocabulary. That development will vary very greatly indeed from child to child according to its circumstances. There are children whose parents do so much for them that they get along very well without using many words. There are other parents so thoroughly neglectful that their children have little opportunity of learning to speak. It is normal, however, for a child in a reasonably good home to have acquired a vocabulary of a hundred or two meaningful sounds (many of them accurately pronounced words) by the end of the second year.

Speaking Vocabularies.

At the age of eighteen months A had, I estimated, a vocabulary of about sixty words. When she was twenty-three months old I made an attempt to write down every word she had been heard to use meaningfully and with fairly accurate pronunciation. The result was the following list. It is a minimum list. I have omitted all proper names whether of people, towns, streets, or characters in stories and nursery rhymes. In the main, derived words like *shopping* from *shop* have been excluded. So also purely repetitive words, e.g. the numbers 3-20:

A vocabulary at 23 months.

a, air, all, an, and, any, apple, away; bacon, bag, ball, banana, basket, bath, bathroom, bear, bed, big, bike, bird, biscuit, bit, blanket, book, bottle, box, boy, bread, brush, bucket, bus, buy, bye-bye; cake, car, card, careful, carrot, carry, castle, cat, catch, chair, chalk, chocolate, clean, clock, club, coat, coal, cocoa, come, cough, cow, crooked, cupboard; daddy, dangerous, day, diamond, dinner, dining-room, dog, door, down, draw, dress, drink, dry, duck; ear, egg, eyes; far, fasten, feet, find, finger, fire, floor, flower, flour, foot, for, fork, found, from; garden, gate, get, girl, glasses, gloves, go, golly, good; had, hair, hand, hard, hat, head, hello, hen, high, horse, hot, house; I, in, is, it; jam, jelly, jump, jumper; kettle, kitchen, knife; laces, lady, lavatory, leg, leggings, letter, letter-box, lid, lie, light, lightning, like, look; make, man, matter, milk, milkman, mine, moon, more, Mrs., mummy; nail, name, nappy, neck, nice, no, now; on, one, open, orange; paint, pants, paper, parcel, peg, pencil, pick, picture, pie, pin, pipe, plane (aeroplane), plasticine, please, pocket, pony, potato, patty, powder, pram, pudding, purse, pussy, put, pyjamas; queen; radio, rain, reins, ride, road, rolling-pin, room, run; salt, sand, sandpit, sandwich, see, shining, shoe, shop, shut, sing, sit, sky, slip, smoke, sneeze, snow, spoon, square, stairs, steps, strap, suit, sun, swing; table, ta-ta, tea, teddy, telephone, the, thank, that, thunder, tin, to, tomato, top, too, tree, two; umbrella, under, up; van; waken, walk, want, water, weather-cock, wet, what, where, white, windmill, window, window-cleaner, wireless; you, your. (247 words).

Children about this stage turn into 'little chatterboxes'. C. K. Ogden has stated that about this time a child will speak as many as 20,000 words in a day. How many different words are there in those 20,000? In order to gain an impression of this on one particular day, five weeks before A's third birthday, I noted every word I heard her use between getting up in the morning and going to bed at night. This produced the following list:

All in a day at 35 months.

A, again, all, an, and, another, are, aren't, away; back, bacon, ball, banana, basket, bell, bend, beside, better, big, biscuit, blackboard, bonfire, book, both, box, bread, breakfast, bring, brought, bump, bus, busy, butter, button; can, cardigan, chair, chin, Christmas, cigarette, clap, clean, clever, clothes, coal, coat, cocoa, come, could, cup, cut; daddy, dance, did, dinner, do, dog, doll, don't, down, draw, drink, drop; empty; face, feel, fell, find, fire, first, floor, for, frock, front; get, girl, give, go, good, goose, grilled; hand, harden, hat, have, he, help, him; I, is, in, it; jam, juice; kettle, kitchen; late, letter, lie, light, like, little, look, lose, lot; made, making, man, manage, marmalade, matches, me, microphone, might, milk, mincer, mine, moment, mummy, my; naughty, need, nice, no, noddle-box, not, now; off, on, one, open, out; paper, pencil, penny, pick, piece, piggies, place, plate, play, please, pussy, put; reach, read, ready, right, roof, room, rosebush, rough, round; sandwich, say, saw, scissors, see, shall, shoe, should, sit, skin, sleep, smack, smell, some, somewhere, spoon, stand, stood, steps, sugar, sweet; table, take, taste, tea, telephone, thank, the, there, things, this, those, though, toe, together, told, tomorrow, touch, toy, try, tummy, turn; under, upstairs; want, warm, was, wash, watch, we, weather-cock, wet, what, where, window, with, wonder, word, would, write; vacuum-cleaner, very; we, wee; yes, you, your, yours. (221 words).

What about the child of school age? Seashore estimated the vocabulary of the 6-7 year old in America as 16,000 basic words and 8,000 derived words, but few educationists have accepted an estimate so high. Probably the most reliable estimate is that of A. F. Watts in *Language and the Mental Development of Children* who wrote:

The average child enters a public elementary school at five with a vocabulary of at least two thousand words (ample for any educational adventure with an intelligent teacher).

He also records, however, that when 200 teachers were asked to estimate the average speaking vocabulary of a five year old, more than half of them gave an estimate of less than two hundred words and over two-thirds gave an estimate of less than three hundred words. None went as high as 2,000 and the median estimate of the whole group was 175 words. I have myself tested these teacher estimates with twenty-three groups of teachers with very similar results. There are two obvious reasons for these low estimates: (1) children talk less in school than they do outside it (2) teachers are very probably influenced in their estimates by the fact that a five-year-old has so limited a reading vocabulary if indeed he has any at all.

Few and Frequent.

The creator of reading-books for the first stages, then, has no lack of words to choose from when he is freed from the old phonic limitations. Among the 2,000 words to choose from there is plenty of variety of visual structure to enable Schonell's principle to be observed too. The children in schools, it might now have been thought, could look forward to reading books full of absorbing stories at the very first stage. But did they? They did not. Pick up any primer which claims to have 'a scientifically controlled vocabulary' and you find, not a story, but a series of dull repetitive sentences which anyone could string together in a matter of minutes.

Look!
Look! Look!
Look, Peter!
My new bicycle.
A red bicycle.
Look, Mary!
I can ride.
I can ride my bicycle.
I can ride my new bicycle.
I can ride my new red bicycle.
Yes, Peter, you may ride.
You may ride my bicycle, Peter.
You may ride my new bicycle.
It is a red bicycle.

With a few more rearrangements of the same words and an artist to supply pictures to excite interest and add meaning, there is a modern-style primer fitted. For the exciting word *bicycle* is now permissible.

The trouble was that a new principle had become necessary. It is all right having the word *bicycle* in the context I have put it in. It is

118

easily recognised as 'the long one' or 'the big one'. Put two long ones in the same book, however, and the difficulty is more than doubled for the child. The plain fact is that, unless the vocabulary is even more limited than the most old-fashioned phonic ones were, the labour of teaching and learning words as wholes is infinitely greater than the task of distinguishing between words by knowing what letters are in them, what order the letters are in, and why these letters are there in that particular order.

It was because of the inherent difficulty of accurate recognition by general shape that the new principle of vocabulary control was evolved. It may be called the 'few-and-frequent' principle which was that of writing a book using as few words as possible and using each of these words as often as possible while still retaining a vestige of sense and observing the subsidiary principle of not introducing more than one new word on a page. *The McKee Readers* mentioned in Chapter XI which were brought to this country from America in 1955 are the outstanding example of this kind of book easily available in this country. The total vocabulary of the first book is twenty words. The reading matter in the first few pages goes like this:

Page

1. Tip.

2. Tip, Tip.

3. No, Tip.

4. No, Tip,
   No, No.

5. Here, Tip.

6. Here, Tip,
   Here, Here.

The meaningful context is 'scientifically' supplied by the pictures.

So, having started out to teach children to read by keeping letters away from them at the first stages, the theory of word-wholes ended up by keeping as many words away from them as possible.

In the *Times Educational Supplement* of 7th June, 1959, J. C. Gagg wrote:

The time seems to have come when the important question to ask when considering a word is: 'How often does a young child use it?' Subsidiary but also relevant questions should be: 'How often does a young child hear it?' and 'How full of interest is it?' Words which appear in a favourable light in answer to these questions should surely be the first choice in preparing reading-matter for the first stages of reading. Then, and only then, should considerations of length, shape, and phonic development be applied to the planning of the eventual material.

In this connexion we have an excellent guide in the research edited by Burroughs. In it, we learn that among the 500 most common words actually used in speech by children about to learn to read are *aeroplane, colour, because, penknife, porridge, elephant, cupboard, once, orange, picture, chimney, people, mirror, night,* and many similar familiar but constructionally difficult words. These make contrasting but exciting reading alongside *Pat is in the pit* and there can be no doubt which type of word should be used with children in these more enlightened days.

This is certainly an attractive theory and here most persuasively expressed. This is the aspect of word-whole theory which has most persuaded teachers in England to turn away from phonics at the early stages. Unfortunately, much as one might wish to agree with a theory which appears to be so much on the side of the child, the argument is specious, even the appeal to Burroughs' research is specious.

The study of vocabulary has many social, educational and psychological implications in this U and non-U world. But where does the naiveté come from which suggests that a selection of the words for first readers is made more authentic because the speaking vocabularies of children at school have been diligently recorded and tabulated? If meaning, use, and interest were the only criteria there is not a parent of any three-year-old child who could not on the spur of the moment reel off scores of words that are absolutely necessary for the first reading-book: *ice-cream, bicycle, ball, chocolate, holidays, snow-man, Christmas, sea-side.*

Another piece of specious arguing is in the suggestion that the alternative to the use of these exciting words is to put rather dull and meaningless sentences in front of the child. If a writer set his mind to it, good and interesting stories can be written for children with the very minimum of irregularly spelt words. This was a task J. C. Daniels and I set ourselves in the early books of the *Royal Road Readers.* The

120

First Companion Books in that series contain complete little stories with only one word in them in which each letter does not stand for a single consistent sound—the word *the*. But the essential fallacy in the argument is that of assuming that one can load early reading-books with words so familiar, so interesting, yet so 'structurally difficult' and get children who cannot yet read to read them. What escaped the writer of the passage quoted was that the few-and-frequent principle was a necessary concomitant of word-whole theory, forced upon the experts by the nature of the child's perceptual and intellectual processes. This is why the new-style reading-books fell so dismally short of their promise in every way except their lay-out and illustrations. No amount of research into the words children use can do anything about this, for all it can show that has any connection with reading-books is how vast a child's speaking vocabulary is compared with the vocabulary of a first reading-book of any practicable size, no matter on what principle constructed. The frequent claim that the release from phonic limitations enabled the publishers to produce books more directly related to the child's spoken vocabulary is best looked at in the context of facts. The most relevant facts are that it is made a selling-point of such books to have a vocabulary limited to 20-30 words and these books are intended for children of six, the American school-entry age, who have an average speaking vocabulary of 3,000—4,000 words at a cautious estimate. It is a corrective thought, too, that many a child of twelve months has a speaking vocabulary of more than twenty words and that a child of three may use several times that number in almost any half-hour during a day in which as many as 20,000 running words may come tumbling off his tongue.

Part Four

ROCKS
BENEATH THE
SHIFTING SANDS

Chapter XIII

LETTERS HAVE MEANINGS

This is the shortest chapter in the book. The chapter itself may be said to be at the head of this page: *Letters have meanings.* The following sentences are an extended foot-note to it.

The idea that letters have meanings is an extremely simple one. Anyone who has not had his mind confused by too much theorising knows this to be so as soon as he thinks about the matter. Normally, however, we do not have to think about letter-meanings because our concern is habitually with the meanings of words. When we say of a speaker, 'I could not following his meaning', it is obviously his word-meanings we are referring to. Anyway, speakers do not use letters. When we say of a piece of written English, 'I can't get the meaning of this paragraph', it is again the meaning of the words we are referring to, even though there are many more letters than words in the paragraph. This is all very well in ordinary usage, in every context except that of teaching reading. But it is precisely in books and articles on the teaching of reading that one meets the statement that letters have no meaning.

> Since meaning lies in groups of words, and not so much in single words (and not at all in letters) reading-teaching should never stress letters and sounds.

Although that sentence sounds as though it were taken direct from an American book of the post-nineteen thirties, it comes from one of a series of articles presenting the modern view of teaching reading which ran for three months in the *Schoolmaster*, official organ of the National Union of Teachers in England, in 1957. The articles were anonymous but a journal of such official standing is hardly likely to have run a series of articles by anyone not regarded as an accredited expert, and indeed the articles were substantially the same as the chapters of a book published later by one of the liveliest educational journalists in England, J. C. Gagg. In making that statement about the meaning-lessness of letters the writer was echoing what had been said many times by more academic educationists, for this is one of the common-places of the literature on this subject. At the same time it is one of the clearest examples of confused thinking in the history of ideas about teaching reading.

The idea had its origin in the incompatible marriage of two similar facts: (1) We usually use 'meaning' in relation to words. (2) Children do recognise words in print and say them correctly before they know anything about letters.

Children come to school equipped with a considerable number of word-meanings. Because of their ability to recognise some of the words whose meanings they already know without having any knowledge of letters, it *is* possible for them to get the meaning out of some printed sentences without any letter-knowledge. In a sense then it can be said that children can read without knowing the letters and that therefore letters have no meaning for them and need not have meaning for them to begin reading. But to use the word 'read' to describe what children are doing in such a case is to give it a somewhat different meaning from the one it has when we say that someone can *read*.

The two meanings of 'read' which are involved here are:

(1) Getting speech-meanings from printed words even while having only a vague perception of these words and having no idea at all as to why they should look as they do.

(2) Getting meanings from printed words on the basis of a sufficient knowledge of letters not only to know which letters are there and why they are there in that particular order but also to know *from the letters and their order* which word in their speaking vocabulary is represented in print even though they have never seen that particular arrangement of letters before.

Most word-whole advocates do draw a distinction between these two types of reading, by referring to the second as 'real reading'. What they consistently fail to bring out is the fact that the essential difference between the two types of reading is that the 'real reader' knows what letters are, what they look like individually, what they mean in terms of sound and what the order in which they appear means. It is the glossing over of this essential difference, added to the use of the word 'read' for the vague recognition stage and to our customary use of the 'meaning' to stand for word-meanings, that has enabled the experts to jump from the fact that letters are meaningless to children who read, but not 'really read', to the fiction that letters have not any meaning at all.

It is not quite enough to say that letters mean sounds, for this does not fully bring out the fact that letters have meanings. A letter is in fact a written or printed sign conveying instructions as to the use of the voice muscles; the order of the letters in the printed word conveys information as to the order in which these instructions are carried out. If you see a grouping of letters that is new to you, e.g. *stulliolb* you have no difficulty in carrying out the instructions and producing the same sounds as everyone else would, because you have learned the conventional letter-meanings, or, to use a term that is creeping into use, signification. These letters convey instructions quite as definitely as the command, 'Quick march!' does.

The fact that the letter-conveyed instructions are so often carried out in the concealment of inner speech, as when we are reading silently, helps us to forget there are any instructions there at all.

To be fully aware of the existence of letter-meanings, however, is to see the full absurdity of some of the statements that are made. The corollary to the statement that letters have no meaning for young children is not that letters have no meaning at all, but that the best means possible should be devised to teach the children that letters have meanings and to teach him what those meanings are—because this is the crucial stage in learning to read—the stage in fact of insight, in the fullest sense of the term.

Great care was taken to ensure that in reading books only words the child already knew the meaning of were used, and used in sentences so simple that the child could not fail to understand them. Yet the constant argument was that children were to be taught to get meaning from the printed words. Having made certain there was nothing the child could not understand, you proceeded to teach him to understand it. But in fact what was happening was that the child, often behind the expert's back, was learning that the words he was so familiar with in speech looked as they did in print because of the letters in them and that there was a reason for the letters being there—they meant something.

Chapter XIV

MEASURING READING ABILITY

I have suggested that it is difficult to be very precise in writing about how Gestalt theory has influenced the teaching of reading because so many influences were simultaneously at work. It is doubtful if word-recognition tests as such were evolved as a result of Gestalt-based ideas, but it is certain that it was as a result of the complex of ideas of which Gestalt psychology was part that word-recognition tests acquired their now familiar characteristics. There emerged, in theory, a new order of difficulty in words to be read—indeed, a new principle of difficulty.

In the days when the alphabetic method was in the ascendant it was held that, meaning apart, the shorter a word was the easier it was to read; in the days of the traditional phonic method this idea persisted with the rider that in addition the easiest words to read were those which were regularly spelt. When Gestalt theory was brought to bear on this matter, however, the idea was generated that the easiest words were those which had a 'distinctive shape'. Length and spelling complexity were no longer taken into account.

In the word-recognition test of the Gestalt era the grading of the words is according to the frequency of correct responses by the sample of children who provided the data for standardisation. The application of the most vigorous statistical techniques will not, however, produce a satisfactory measuring instrument if some of the fundamental premises are themselves unsatisfactory. This is what happens with word-recognition tests graded in this way. The fundamental misconception or assumption is that the child who correctly responds to the printed word *tree* by saying 'tree', is perceiving the word *tree* in the same way as the adult does. We have seen, however, that there is a possibility that the child's perception of the word is of a very different quality. It may well be that he says 'tree' for no other reason than that he has associated that spoken word with a set of markings upon paper out of which he has clearly discriminated *ee* and so he might equally likely have responded with 'tree' if the word *free* had been presented to him. It is also to be noted that selecting items in a test of this type is very much a function of the type of teaching the pupils have had. The word *tree* is the first word in the Schonell word-recognition test not because it is intrinsically an easier word to read than *I* or *a* but because in the particular type of teaching the children had been given, or because in the books they had been using, the word *tree* had frequently occurred. It does not, however, necessarily follow that this word occurred more frequently than the words *little* and *milk* which appear next in the Schonell test, for it may well have been that the pupils found the *ee* of *tree* more easily memorable than any of the details of the other words they were required to read in the draft test material. Tests of this kind no doubt have a certain value as measuring instruments, but this value is not apparent at the lower levels of achievement. If, for example, we consider the child who has a reading age of six on this test, we find that he has been able to say the first ten words of the test correctly, but we have no information as to whether he would not have said those same words if he had been shown similar words such as *free*, *milk*, *kettle* and so on. The more words a child responds to correctly in this way, of course, the more likely it is that he is perceiving the words as the skilled adult does, for the number of printed words that a child can respond to correctly when he perceives only parts of them is limited, and it is highly improbable that a child will be able to emerge from such a test with a reading age of eight without having considerable insight into the function of letters. Word recognition, however, is a problem only with children who have made little progress in reading. What we wish to know about children who can already read is not whether they recognise words but whether they understand them and this is something which the word-recognition test does not set out to do. What the word-recognition test does give is some measure of the child's familiarity with the printed word. This is to say, after the first twenty words or so it functions as a measure of the child's reading experience. At the lower levels of achievement it has little of significance to say. It does not give statistically accurate measures of achievement (see G. F. Reed, *Studies in Education*, University College of Hull, Volume II, No. 1, 1953 and *Reading Ability*, Ministry of Education 1950) nor can it give precise information about the pupil's power of word recognition.

It is unfortunately with the younger and least successful pupils that such tests are most often used because it is about them chiefly that the kind of information such a test purports to give is most often required. Whether the existence of tests of this kind has had much direct influence upon the kind of teaching done in schools it is difficult to say. One may perhaps suggest that, by enabling teachers to give 'reading ages' to pupils who cannot read but have merely by some undefined means recognised a few words, these tests have helped to obscure failure and given apparently scientific evidence of success where there has been little or none. It is also possible, since at the early stages they are so inaccurate an instrument, that they have given evidence of failure where in fact there has been success. A child who has been taught by some variety of phonic method may be able to read a large number of words of the 'sit', 'bun', 'man', type but may never have met the first two words in the test—*tree* and *little*. Can one be sure that the pattern of failure in the test established with the first few words does not affect his responses even to the regularly phonic words later in the test which in more normal circumstances he can read?

The purpose of a test of this sort is to give the teacher, in a matter of minutes, information which it would otherwise take him some time to acquire. In the hands of a teacher who is aware of its weaknesses as a measuring instrument this result will be achieved, but only with those pupils who register a reading age of about 7 or more, for the reasons already indicated.

Before the twentieth century it was not generally held that children could be said to be able to read unless they had acquired skill in recognition of letters and insight into the function of letters. The type of word-recognition test I have been discussing assumes that the recognition of words by any means whatsoever is *reading*. It is more in keeping with the theory of word-perception put forward in this study to say that the ability to recognise a few words in the manner required by this kind of test is an indication that the child has made some progress towards reading. He may be said to be at the later part of the pre-reading stage. So what is described as a reading-age of, say 5.5, would be more accurately described as a pre-reading age.

An attempt to produce a series of tests which would give a teacher more information about a child's progress in 'real reading' was made by J. C. Daniels and I in *The Standard Reading Tests*. The key test in the battery is 'The Standard Test of Reading Skill' which, while being a test of a child's ability to read running text with understanding, is fundamentally a foot-rule measuring how much a child has learned about the various sound-meanings letters have in our irregularly spelt language.

The first item in this reading-skill test is:

Can a dog run?

The last is:

Which of the following can be bought at a chemist's?

Dough-mixing machines; faulty refrigerators; cough mixture; physical energy.

Between these two items there is a grading of phonic complexity. So the point a pupil reaches on this scale is a measure of what he has learned about English letter-meanings, knowledge without which he cannot possibly know why any particular word looks as it does in print.

131

Chapter XV

HOW THINGS STAND TODAY

Since the twenties the very extensive literature on the subject of reading has been so heavy with Gestalt terminology and has remained so well within the circle of Gestalt thinking that it all creates a strong impression that this school of psychology brought about a revolution in the teaching of reading. Our closer examination of the history of this topic has, however, shown that it did no such thing. We found that in the first half of the nineteenth century Josiah Bumstead and John Russell Webb, in America, had separately devised books designed on a sketchy word-whole principle. To them the principle was a very simple one. They said in effect: 'Learning the letters is a bore. We've noticed that children will recognise words before they know the letters. Let's skip the letter drill and start with the words'.

At the end of the nineteenth century Farnham, also in America, was theorising about reading, in sentences that are indistinguishable from Gestalt writing on the subject. The conclusion one draws is that both word-whole teaching as a worked out theory and Gestalt psychology as an established school arose about the same time out of the same climate of thought. What happened later was that educational psychologists took what they wanted from Gestalt theory and used it to give apparently fully accredited scientific support to practices that were already in being. Nothing in the history of teaching reading is quite so clear-cut as all that, however. It does very much look, for example, as though Schonell, who in his theory was so much dominated by Gestalt thinking, did sincerely believe that the new psychology had brought really new and valid concepts to the teaching of reading.

By the late 1940's reading books constructed on the principles of whole psychology were firmly established in the great majority of schools throughout the English-speaking world. Their vocabularies were 'scientifically controlled' on the few-and-frequent and sometimes difference-of-structure principle. In England and the British Common-wealth the most popular of these was the *Janet and John* series, a favourite in schools in England and South Africa and almost universally used a year or two ago in New Zealand, but not quite so popular in the country of its origin, the United States, not because it did not fall in with theoretical requirements there but because it had to compete with so many others which in illustration, lay-out and meaning and vocabulary content were almost indistinguishable—the *Dick and Jane* readers, the *Bruce and Barbara* readers—even the titles followed the same pattern.

In the brief outline of the earlier history of the teaching of reading I quoted a passage from W. S. Gray indicating the extremes to which word-whole theory was driven in the United States. In few schools in England and fewer schools in Scotland did such extreme practices obtain. In the immediate post-war years, however, there was consider-able public concern about the number of backward readers not only in the primary schools but in the secondary modern schools too. Public attention was drawn to this by complaints from the Army about illiteracy among the young men conscripted for national service. The disruption of family life and of the school system itself was perhaps enough to account for as much illiteracy as the Army authorities discovered. Yet there were many teachers, particularly those concerned with backward readers, who, finding that what backward readers mostly required was a knowledge of the letters, felt critical of the theory which paid so much attention to whole words at the early stages and so little attention to letters.

In 1954 J. C. Daniels and I through the *News Chronicle* published a pamphlet called *Learning to Read*. We had previously contributed a few articles to the educational press and our ideas had been the subject of a heated controversy in the *News Chronicle* itself. The pamphlet was distributed free to delegates at the annual general conference of the N.U.T. in 1954 and attracted a good deal of attention in the educational press.

The ideas put forward in that pamphlet were briefly: that an alphabet is a way of writing down the sounds of speech, that the order of letters in a word signifies an order of time, that the idea that children see words as immediate wholes is based on careless observation of

133

children who can be observed in the process of analysing the words, that the 'general shape' of a word is purely adventitious, that the only logical visual analysis of printed words is into letters, that in learning to read children are in fact learning to translate symbols of sounds (letters) into blocks of sound that make sense. We then outlined a set of teaching material which would fit in with these ideas. This teaching material was later published by Chatto and Windus as the *Royal Road Readers*, the first books appearing in 1954.

Although we continually insisted on the supremacy of letters in learning to read, we did not in this teaching material begin with the alphabet. Our reason was that letters were too abstract for the very first stage. On the other hand we rejected the idea of choosing words for their difference of visual structure because this was leading the child away from letters. So our first exercises were with three-letter words only—those referred to in the chapter on the perception of words. We made it clear, both in the pamphlet and in the *Teacher's Book* accompanying the readers, that we did not expect pupils to begin with our scheme on the first day in school but that on the contrary a good deal of play-way practice in listening to words as in the 'I-Spy' game and in looking at and talking about pictures and so on should first be given. The whole aim of the teaching material was to lead the child as quickly as possible towards insight into the significance of letters. To this end we limited the number of letter-meanings the child had to deal with by using only phonically simple words at the first stage, but we took care to see that at every single part of the scheme the pupils had to deal with word-meanings as well.

The controversy which these various publications stirred up does not yet seem to have died down. Yet a change appears to be working. In fact it seems as though, just as word-whole theory became articulate in the climate of thought which gave rise to Gestalt theory, so a reversion to a theory of teaching reading more in keeping with the nature of alphabetic writing appears to be taking place in the climate of thought which has led to the decline of Gestalt theory. This more recent development has, I think, its roots in the great amount of work that has been done in semantics since the publication in 1924 of Ogden and Richards' *The Meaning of Meaning*. The sloppy thinking which allows reading specialists to say that letters have no meaning cannot comfortably co-exist alongside the careful work that has resulted in present-day theories of signs and 'significs'.

The criticism of word-whole theory was not confined to this country.

Towards the end of 1954 I was invited by the Johannesburg branch of New Education Fellowship to lecture in various centres in the Union. One of the reasons for the invitation was the publication of *The Global Reading Method* which is quoted on page 84.

A considerable number of teachers in that country, I discovered, were in mild revolt against the official view expounded in that publication—within two hours of stepping off the boat at Cape Town I was asked by the literary editor of the *Cape Times* whether I was one of those people who advocated the teaching of reading as though English were Chinese!

Meanwhile a far hotter controversy flared up in America with the publication in March 1955 of *Why Johnny Can't Read* by Rudolf Flesch. The book was addressed to parents and was in the best-selling lists in America for over thirty weeks. In spite of this kind of success, *Why Johnny Can't Read* was in other ways a failure. It was as if Flesch had seized the barrel of a blunderbuss and laid about him at all the educationists he could find. Beside this book anything J. C. Daniels and I had written on the subject was like mild gossip over a weak cup of tea. Unfortunately Flesch left himself wide open to attacks for he advocated in effect a simple return to teaching the letters. He was, however, less well-informed about why it was a good thing to teach the letters than his enemies were about why it was not. The result of this book was that the American educationists and many teachers came together in mass counter-attack. The book had been serialised in the *San Francisco Examiner*; the Californian Teachers' Federation took over two pages of the paper to deliver a counterblast. The University of Chicago each year hold a large conference on reading; it was devoted entirely to 'The Flesch Controversy', Arthur I. Gates by then a venerable figure, himself produced a pamphlet called *Johnny and his Reading*. America in fact seethed with the controversy and the upshot was that word-whole theory was more firmly established in the minds of educationists than before.

In the following year J. C. Daniels and I, through the Institute of Education of Nottingham University published *Progress in Reading*, a comparative study of the efficiency of two methods of teaching reading. Work on this project had begun when a headmaster wrote saying he would like us to see the progress his backward pupils were making using the *Royal Road Readers*. The two methods being compared were the 'mixed methods' which can be said to be normal in English schools today (i.e. 'whole-word reading-books' and in the teaching a mixture of word recognition by wholes eked out with incidental phonics) and the method of the *Royal Road Readers*, now known as the Phonic Word Method. A considerable amount of delving into past work of a similar kind led to this conclusion:

> The large measure of agreement in the experimental evidence showing the superiority of various types of phonic method to various 'whole word', 'sentence' and other 'modern' methods is surprising in view of the general trend of expert and official opinion.

The pupils who were studied in this piece of research were all the pupils in four junior schools who had entered those schools with so little idea of reading that not one of them made any score at all in the word recognition tests used in the schools. This was after they had had two years in infant schools using 'mixed methods'. The percentages of the pupils entering the four schools with this low level of achievement were respectively 27.5, 34.3, 15.4 and 22.2 giving an average percentage of 26.1. The main advantage of rigidly choosing pupils so completely illiterate is that it largely cuts out the influence of the home. The teaching of reading is an activity which many parents feel they must take part in with, for research-workers, the unfortunate result that no matter how carefully things are planned and executed in the school the conclusions of the experiments in so far as they state that such a result was due to the school are always suspect because it is so difficult to account for what might have been happening in the home. It seemed to us reasonable to assume that a child who had been two years at an infant school without being able to recognise a simple word at the end of it was not likely to have had much help from his parents. At any rate, if they had had any help, it could hardly be said to have made much difference. It also seemed to us that the factor of intelligence was taken care of because after all about three-quarters of the age-group had learned to read under the same school, though perhaps different, home conditions as those who had so signally failed. Other details were taken care of as far as it was possible to do so, e.g. the socio-economic status of the schools and the experience of the teachers. At the end of the first junior year the pupils were tested with a series of tests half of which favoured the 'mixed method' pupils, the other half favouring the phonic word method pupils. In the four word recognition tests the average number of correct responses were:

Phonic word method ..	75%
Mixed methods.. ..	43%

One of the surprising results was that the 'mixed method' pupils had a higher score in the test composed of words from Book I of the *Royal Road Readers* than in the test composed of words chosen from the various word-whole readers used in their school. To the lay mind it would hardly seem necessary to prove that short phonically simple words are the easiest of all to read, but the history as set forth in this book suggests that, since the incredible had been lodged so firmly in people's minds by elaborate research and theorising, the obvious could be reinstated only by a similar process of elaborate inquiry.

I have selected from the lists of results in *Progress in Reading* the ten words in the single-word tests which the phonic word method pupils found easiest, easy being judged on the single statistic of number of correct responses. Opposite each word I give first the percentage of pupils in the phonic word method group (A) who read the word correctly and then the corresponding percentage for the mixed method pupils (B). Alongside this list I give the corresponding list of words found easiest by the mixed method pupils. Again the first column of figures refers to the phonic word method pupils.

EASIEST WORDS

Phonic Word Method			Mixed Method		
	A	B		A	B
will	95	83	boy	91	91
went	95	69	will	95	83
ask	94	56	girl	89	80
fell	94	47	milk	89	80
lost	91	50	you	91	80
boy	91	91	ball	91	78
you	91	80	little	87	78
ball	91	78	milkman	89	77
get	90	71	play	87	76
across	90	71	get	90	71

For reasons connected with the construction of the tests the words *red* and *cut* each occurred in two of the tests. The scores for these two words varied slightly. If I had taken the best score for these words both of them would have appeared in the first list and *red* would have appeared in the second. The average of the scores kept both out of both lists by a hair's breadth. All the words, it is noticeable, are monosyllabic except *milkman* and *across*, and these are regularly phonic.

Similar lists of the words found most difficult in the tests are now given.

MOST DIFFICULT WORDS

Phonic word method pupils			Mixed method pupils		
	A	B		A	B
through	37	21	attract	66	7
laugh	41	16	board	73	15
figure	44	15	curtains	64	15
answer	47	17	figure	44	15
brought	48	24	laugh	41	16
high..	50	21	aeroplane	51	16
aeroplane	51	16	husband	72	16
know	52	42	answer	47	17
beautiful	56	24	thought	44	17
once	57	36	different	80	18

It appears from this that irregularly spelt words are the most difficult for all pupils no matter what the method taught. It is interesting to note that *aeroplane*, which occurs in the first book of the *Janet and John* series and which a large number of these pupils had been 'seeing' off and on for three years occurs in both lists. It will be noted that in no case does the B score exceed the A score and that only in the word *boy* did the B percentage equal the A. There was in fact among the 80 words no instance of the B score exceeding the A.

Some of the items were surprising in the extent of the difference between the groups. Two such items occur in the lists given—*across* and *different*. Other surprising items are:

	A	B		A	B
but	89	38	step	84	34
himself	88	22	plank	82	38
hundred	80	25	kennel	78	37

There were fewer such gross differences among the less regular words, yet the following are sufficiently striking:

	A	B		A	B
use	65	30	young	71	32
talk	60	24	find	78	40
four	74	48	board	73	15

The most striking thing, however, about the results of the single-word tests was the number of silences on the part of the 'mixed method' pupils. No less than 46 per cent. of their responses were blank silences; 16 per cent. was the corresponding figure for the phonic word method pupils. The results of the sentence tests followed the same pattern as those of the single-word tests. In a test of eight simple phonic sentences the phonic word method pupils had on the average 4.6 correct readings compared with 1.9 in the other group. In sentences compiled from the vocabulary of word-method primers the phonic word method pupils averaged 4.1 correct to the mixed method score of 2.6.

Errors in Reading.

All the responses of the pupils had been recorded on tape and this enabled us to carry out the laborious task of studying the types of error made by the pupils. Every wrong reading is recorded in phonetic script in *Progress in Reading*.

These errors form a weird collection. In studying previous work on this aspect of reading we found again that Gestalt theory had led some research-workers to conclusions that did not seem to us valid, in particular the frequent statement that a large proportion of children's errors in reading are due to confusion of general shape. It is easy to reach this conclusion if one underestimates the role of visual analysis of words or pays too scant attention to a child's habit of fixing upon details. H. Frank, for example, in a study printed in the *British Journal of Educational Psychology* in 1935 gave 'similarity of structure' as the reason for confusion between *foot* and *forest* and for the following attempts to write shop: *sop, sho, tholp, hop, shok, soy.* It is just as reasonable to say that the child who read *foot* for *forest* did so because he saw that the word he was trying to read began with *fo* and ended with *t* and the word most familiar to him which had these characteristics was *foot*. There is certainly something in the idea that words similar in general structure will be confused. If I had stopped at *ocvc* instead of carrying on to complete *ocvcglomc* the pupils I mentioned earlier would not have shouted out 'Aeroplane'. Unfortunately for the theory, however, words that are regarded as of similar structure are also words that have some letters in common and if due attention is paid to the facts about perception set out in Chapter 10 one is forced to the conclusion that it is in general more accurate to say that a pupil has seen part of one word, say one or two letters, and has associated what he has seen with another and probably more familiar word which contains the same letters. The conclusions we reached after our study of the numerous errors made by those children were that the most frequent cause of error was part-seeing of the print in front of them and whole-saying of a word they had part-seen elsewhere. The part of a word children gave greatest attention to was usually the first letter or two; the middle letters were given less attention than any other part of the word. The mixed method pupils who had had less training in accurate visual perception were, as might be expected, much more prone than the others to make mistakes of this kind. From the 'mixed methods' group there came some interesting renderings of the sentence, 'The hens clucked':

The has chimly.	The hine clickle.
The hands chicked.	The hansh chiskid.
The hangs kangs.	The hens chickens.

The last is particularly interesting when one considers the inter-relationship between 'inner speech' and perception. It seems likely that, having read the word *hens* and immediately thereafter having to deal with the retinal image of a word so similar in 'general structure' to *chickens*, the pupil saw *chickens* as clearly on the page in front of him as he ever saw it in his life—this may not have been very clear but it was clear enough to produce an interesting mistake. How many pupils saw only part of a word and said the right one we shall never know.

This report attracted a good deal of attention and continues to do so. Professor D. H. Russell, some of whose work is referred to in an earlier chapter, reviewed it at great length in the American journal *Elementary English*. The briefest note, and from the lay point of view the most sensible, appeared in the *Daily Sketch* which in three or four lines said in effect that two research-workers at the University of Nottingham after months of work had proved that short simply spelt words were easier to read than long words with complicated spelling.

Other Recent Research.

The Ministry of Education has since the war, published several surveys of standards of reading. In the first of these an attempt was made to compare post-war with pre-war standards. It was a difficult thing to do and the research team were not very confident about their conclusions. Nevertheless they did risk saying that reading standards had declined since before the war. Subsequent reports have shown that standards have risen since the immediate post-war years. Much has been made of this in some sections of the educational press but never has any mention been made of the fact that according to the Ministry's own figures the rise in standards has still left the child entering the secondary school well below the standard of his pre-war counterpart. It may be that the calculations were too exposed to the hazards of statistical estimation to be reliable and that the Ministry is content that they should be forgotten. Certainly even the report which contained figures showing junior school leavers of 1955 to be 9 months behind their pre-war counterparts in reading achievement appeared to go out of its way to convince the public that so far as reading was concerned the winds were set fair.

In 1955 the Queensland Department of Public Instruction issued a report giving the results of a study of different methods of teaching reading. Professor Schonell, who had a year or two previously transferred to the Chair of Education at the University of Queensland, had given a series of lectures on modern methods of teaching reading to teachers who were to be engaged in trying out newer methods of teaching reading than were to be found in the schools of Queensland which until then had stuck to a rather old-fashioned phonic method. This old-fashioned method was to be compared with whole-word methods as incorporated in three different sets of reading books, the *Janet and John* readers, the *Happy Venture* readers and a set of readers produced by the Victoria Education Department. After the children had been almost three years at the school they were tested in word recognition, speed of reading, reading comprehension and the ability to attack new words. The result was that the group taught by the old-fashioned phonic method turned out to be superior to all the other groups in all the tests with the solitary and not very happy exception that the *Happy Venture* group had a slight superiority in speed of reading, not very happy because, alongside the lower comprehension scores, it immediately provokes the question: What's the point of reading more quickly if you don't understand what you are reading?

It is one of the great advantages of research into educational problems that these problems are all so very complicated that there is no real need for anyone to accept the results he has so laboriously proved. There is always an emergency exit through which one can dart back to the familiar and reassuring context of prejudices. And quite often reluctance to change one's mind as a result of a few tests is highly commendable because of the very fact that in these research situations there is so great a complexity. So on the face of it Queensland authorities were not at all blame-worthy when they went against their own test results and decided in favour of 'modern' methods on the ground that it improved the children's attitude to reading and this was the most important thing in the long run. Yes, on the face of it—but in fact the Queensland authorities were not merely ignoring their own test results, they were also ignoring the fact that scores of previous studies had ended up with the same sort of results. Their rejection of their own results, however, is not unusual in this field. A diligent and dispassionate student who takes up the subject of reading-research seriously will not have spent many months before he begins to form the opinion that a considerable amount of what has been called research has not been in fact a search for facts as such but a series of attempts to prove scientifically that 'word-whole' or 'modern' methods are superior to letter-based methods. A good deal more has consisted of assertions based upon evidence that has not been revealed. That the proof has still eluded the searchers and researchers is not really daunting to those who are determined to hang on to the concepts of the thirties and forties. There is always an easy answer: namely, that it is inhuman to think that so living a process as learning to read can be scientifically analysed. Reading is not like arithmetic, a mechanical skill built up by the sheer manipulation of symbols: it is part of the child's very personality. This is the current answer to research results of the kind reached in Queensland. And the Queensland authorities countered their own figures in the same vein by their general statement that the child's *attitude* to reading had improved. But in what sense 'improved'? It is one of the commonplaces of 'modern' talk about reading that it is a good thing for the child to be encouraged to think he is reading when he is not 'really reading'. It is possible for a well-intentioned person to believe this to be a good thing only if he at the same time believes that the delight and interest the child has found in pseudo-reading will lead naturally and without conflict into real reading. That is to say, one must believe that saying and seeing, however vaguely, a variety of words regardless of their spelling complexity will lead the child to insight into what alphabetic writing really is. If this belief is not held, one must face up to the fact that at some time in the near future the child will have to accept the shock of discovering that he cannot read after all. It is possible no doubt for a wise and understanding teacher to weaken the shock by making the transition easier, but the wisdom and understanding such a teacher will possess will have come from her personal knowledge of children in the process of learning to read not from the theories which by their prevalence have given rise to this book.

Such pleasant phrases as 'an improved attitude' may conceal the fact that later the child may come up against sharp realities against which his 'improved attitude', because falsely based, provides little defence.

The Kent Report.

I have written at some length about the Queensland researches both because they are fairly recent and also because of a certain similarity they have to the most imposing piece of research into reading published in this country for a long time, research carried out in the county of Kent by the National Foundation for Educational Research and published this year as *Reading in the Primary School*, its author, Dr. Joyce Morris. The similarity between this and the Queensland reports is that here too, phonic methods were found to be superior to others according to the figures but that again conclusions were drawn that ran counter to the statistics. Seldom has such care been taken as in the National Foundation report in the applying of statistical techniques to test results; seldom has such care been taken to explain that the figures so elaborately worked out could not be taken to mean quite what statistically they ought to mean. For example, it was found that among the nine factors examined only two were significant in leading to superiority of reading achievement—the good home ('socio-economic status') and early teaching of phonics. It was pointed out in italics, however, that the high significance of early phonic teaching only emerged after the factor of intelligence had been taken into account. Nothing could be more legitimate, but equally legitimate would have been the statement that in spite of low intelligence on the part of pupils in certain schools, country schools for the most part, the teachers in those schools achieved proportionately better results by their phonic methods than teachers using modern methods did with their more intelligent pupils.

One of the important facts that Dr. Morris omitted to mention in the report is that 'socio-economic status' and early phonic teaching —her two significant factors—are inter-related.

When parents take an interest in, or 'interfere' with, a child's reading, they immediately turn to the letters. Ignorant of word-whole theory, or puzzled or unimpressed by it, they rely on simple phonic teaching. Although I base this statement on observations made outside the Kent area, the same conclusion is implicit in the report itself in the evidence of the headmistress of one of the schools with very high reading scores. This headmistress stated that many of her pupils had already mastered the mechanics of reading by the time they came to school. A mastery of the mechanics of reading implies emphasis upon the letters. Indeed the phrase 'mechanics of reading' is generally used to mean just that, and usually with the implication that there has at the same time been a neglect of the meanings of words. Children who have mastered those mechanics by the comparatively early age of five have almost certainly been taught by a phonic method. This headmistress added that one of her main problems was finding enough reading-books to keep the children interested and had some slightly critical things to say about parents who were so ambitious about their children. Much as she wished to, she had not felt able to use the more modern methods because of the pressure of local public opinion.

The other significant factor associated with high reading ability, early teaching of phonics by the school, was dealt with in slightly more detail in the report. It was quite rightly pointed out that only when statistical allowance was made for intelligence did this factor emerge as of high significance. This qualification was set in italics and is as much as to say: *In spite of the fact that our report is highly statistical and we have taken elaborate care with the statistical calculations, particular caution should be exercised in interpreting this result.* This is a variation of the Queensland method of rejecting results that refuse to conform directly to the accepted prejudices. What the scores actually meant was that those pupils who were of poor intelligence and who were given early phonic teaching produced better scores in reading than their intelligence scores would have led one to expect. They were reading better than they should have done according to the accepted theory of intelligence testing. So, taking the picture as a whole, it would seem that the children of poor intelligence who were taught phonics in school progressed unexpectedly well while many of the best readers of all were those who had had help with phonics at home.

On evidence lending itself to these conclusions, Dr. Morris concluded that word-whole methods were best for the early stages of reading!

Before the report was published, but after it was in print, Dr. Morris surveyed recent research in reading in two articles in the first two issues of the National Foundation's journal, *Educational Research*. In the second of these, February 1959, she summed up her conclusions in the sentence:

> Thus, a synthetic approach to reading, with its emphasis on small, meaningless parts of the words, is likely to be more difficult for most young children than a non-analytical word-whole one.

This is an extraordinary conclusion for someone to reach who had evidence in front of her that children of low intelligence prospered so well by phonic teaching. And yet it is so innocently right, superficially so persuasively true; it so concisely expresses what may be called the official accepted view. Yet it is so fundamentally wrong in its implications.

It is right because there is a difficulty for children in understanding what letters are all about. Meaning, for them, *does* exist in whole spoken words and sentences, not in letters. It is fundamentally wrong, however, in its acceptance of the term 'meaningless' as a description of letters and in its blindness to the fact that the difference between a child who can read and a child who cannot is that for the child who can read letters have acquired specific meanings in terms of sounds to be pronounced or recalled in inner speech. It is wrong in its implication that children who are constantly being shown whole words do not, like the phonically taught children pay attention to meaningless parts of words. On the contrary, as we have seen, they pay attention to and seize upon parts of words that are less meaningful than letters, e.g. *pig* recognised by the dot on the *i*. It is wrong in ignoring the question as to the principle upon which the whole words for teaching are to be chosen, for the type of word chosen affects both the accuracy and the meaningfulness of the child's perception.

Any piece of research which ignores the fact that the significant stage of the process of learning to read is that at which letters are acquiring meaning for the child has a fundamental weakness which an elaboration of statistical techniques may conceal but never do away with. This was evident not only in the conclusions that there were so much in variance with the test results but also in the attempt the National Foundation team made to assess standards. I have set down in Chapter 14 the reasons why word-whole theory produced tests that were of little use with children at the five-to-six year old learning stage. The ineffectiveness of these tests may have been the reason why in the

Kent investigation a different criterion was used. A child was deemed to be 'functionally literate' when he had read Book Four in the series of reading-books in use in the school. The majority of the schools used one of three reading schemes: *Janet and John*, *Happy Venture* and *Beacon*. With this as a criterion it was found that in 1954 the percentage of children in Kent who entered junior schools 'functionally illiterate' was 45. A sample of the rest of the country showed that the standards in Kent were above the national average. The definition of a 'functionally literate child' is a somewhat arbitrary one, but it seems likely that it is effective enough in so far as one can say that a child who has progressed thus far through a reading-scheme will have acquired, whether helped at home or not, a sufficient understanding of letters to be able to tackle a reasonably simple (in the phonic sense) word new to him. Much more useful information would have been obtained, however, by a simple test as to whether a child knew enough about letters and had sufficient confidence in this knowledge to read simple phonic words that did not appear in any of the reading-books. With books constructed on the few-and-frequent principle pupils can go a long way without really getting very far.

The conclusions reached as a result of making this estimate of reading standards were that over half of the children entering the junior school required a continuation of the kind of teaching they had had in the infant school. They were to get more of the mixture as before, the mixture which, if it did not prevent them from learning to read, certainly did not show them how to do it.

Chaos and Cure.

In 1958 there was published in America *Reading: Chaos and Cure* by Sybil Terman and Charles C. Walcutt, a book which showed that the reading controversy was still very much alive in that part of the world. This book attacked the theories of American experts not so acrimoniously but very much more powerfully than Flesch had done in 1955. It was more powerful because it was so much better informed and because it was thought out on a much higher level. It is necessary reading, I would suggest, for anyone in the British Commonwealth who wishes to become informed about the nature and origins of the theories which have affected the lives of so many English-speaking children. The special interest of the book so far as this study is concerned is that at the time of its publication it was unique in the history of reading in critically surveying Gestalt theory in relation to the teaching of reading. Terman and Walcutt pointed out that Gestalt theory was becoming more and more discredited among psychologists generally and showed in some detail that in any case to apply as it had been applied to the teaching of reading was to mis-apply it.

Terman and Walcutt also provided evidence of higher quality than has ever been produced in this country of the decline in standards of reading since the general introduction of word-whole methods to American schools.

One of the classic tests in educational psychology is the Stanford-Binet Intelligence test which first appeared in 1916 and was published in a revised edition in 1931. A third edition is now being prepared by Dr. Maude Merrill James who did most of the work on the second edition. One item in the test requires the pupils to read a paragraph in 35 seconds and to recall eight facts in it with no more than two mistakes. In the first two editions of the test this item was placed at the ten-year-old level, the criterion being that 60 per cent. of the age-group should do it correctly. Dr. James has found, however, that she must now place this item at the twelve-year-old level even though on all other parts of the test the children of today scored the same as those of twenty and forty years ago. So the children of California, educationally one of the most progressive states in America, though of the same average intelligence as their counterparts of twenty and forty years ago, are two years behind in reading achievement—that being measured by the ability to read a paragraph in a set time, understand what was read, and remember what was understood. No one is likely to suggest that the same calamitous state of affairs has come about in this country. One of the reasons is that the teachers in the primary schools of this country are in the main more conservative than their American counterparts and have never as a body been stampeded into forgetting that they are teaching the reading of an alphabetically written language. Another is that in the progressive infant schools of this country reading is not divorced from writing, so that letters come into their own and the children learn to read largely by a spelling method, naming the letters or saying the sounds quietly to themselves as they write or copy them. A third reason is that although American books in an English form are very widely used in this country, teachers are not subjected to the astonishing pressure American teachers suffer from step-by-step advice as to how every page in the chosen book should be used; the common sense which develops in the day-to-day solution of teaching problems impinges upon books in the designing of which common sense was conspicuously lacking.

Chapter XVI

OUTLOOK FOR TOMORROW

Changes in the climate of education do not as a rule take place so quickly that their nature and movement cannot be detected. The most noticeable movement during the twentieth century has been away from the 'subject' and towards the child. Nineteenth century educational methods were subject-dominated; twentieth century education has prided itself on being 'child-centred'. The catch-phrase 'We are teaching children not subjects', which was old when those now starting teaching were young, still echoes through the summer schools and educational conferences and not many of those who utter it realise the ambiguity of the word 'teaching' in that context. For it is impossible merely to teach a child; one must be teaching him *something* if one is teaching him at all.

Now in the second half of the twentieth century it seems likely that a new synthesis is taking place. One must study the nature of the child—to this extent education is child-centred, but one must also study the nature of what the child is required to learn and see it in relation to the processes by which he learns—to this extent education is subject-directed. The reaction against the thought of the past few decades cannot be dismissed as 'the old swing of the pendulum'; the direction is towards a synthesis of a kind not possible in the days of a raw and naive educational psychology.

Whatever changes in theory or practice there may be in the future, however, there are certain facts about the child and his early experience of the printed word which remain constant.

Here are the 'constancies' which may be suggested as the most significant in relation to the knowledge of words written down by means of letters:

(a) However much one may agree with the statement that all children are different—especially one's own—one must also accept the fact that every child who learns to read, unless he is blind or deaf, passes through the same stages.

(b) Once a child has learned to focus his eyes, which is before he has learned to speak, the retinal images in his eyes will frequently contain whole printed words in complete detail. Only rarely and accidentally will the child be conscious of that part of the retinal image. A typical accidental case would be when the child notices neon lights that flash a word. Then he is paying conscious attention to that part of the retinal image which contains the word in its visual form— but to him it is merely a flashing light, not even that quite, for he has not the words to classify in that manner what he sees.

(c) There is a stage during which he is very frequently conscious of print in many different forms and situations. This stage is reached at the same time as he is making noticeable progress in learning to speak, with its consequent increase in acuity of visual perception and fine-ness of discrimination. He is conscious of the printed shapes not as words, not as having any connection with the sounds people make, but simply as marks on hoardings, breakfast cereal packets, occasionally the television screen, and the books or papers the adults around him spend so much time looking at. He will have no idea that there is any connection between the marks on the hoardings and those on the television set or that either of these has any connection with the marks on newspapers or books. He has no clearer a visual image of them than an adult is likely to have of the pattern made by the branches of a tree he saw momentarily silhouetted against the sky.

(d) There is a stage during which the child learns to associate some of these marks with meanings. This stage is entered gradually and often seems to have been entered before it actually has. It may be the colour of a sign and the fact that it is to be seen outside certain shops that gradually leads him to say one day—with the suddenness of Köhler's 'insight'!—'Ice cream!' In the early part of this stage the same trade-name printed in the same colour but against a different background will not so certainly evoke that response. Gradually, however, he will come to the stage when the same sign in the black-and-white of a newspaper advertisement will do so. At the same time other words connected with things of immediate interest to him will acquire this kind of meaning for him in print. It is not, however, the 'general shape' of the word itself which he perceives. There are far too many printed words in the world around him and their general shapes have too great a similarity for him to recognise particular words by this means alone. He seizes upon details and until he meets a situation that upsets his calculations he will be content with any detail however small that serves his purpose, and that purpose is merely to enjoy the pleasure of recognising and repeating something familiar, a pleasure that may have originated in, and is certainly increased by, smiles of pride on the faces of his parents. True, the first impression he has of every printed word every time he sees it is a vague general impression; the vagueness will come to be of very brief duration, however, say a hundredth of a second, not much longer than it takes him to direct his attention in that direction.

(e)   There is a stage where he begins to associate particular parts of printed words with parts of the spoken word—letters come to mean sounds. The irregular spelling of English makes it unlikely that this will take place without guidance of a special character. For a child to discover the relationship for himself in a regularly spelt language would denote an exceptional power of reasoning. A child thus highly endowed who began to see the relationship in English is likely to flounder and become more unsure of himself because of the inconsistency or the letter-meanings. Yet this is the important stage in progress towards skill in reading. Is he to be encouraged to rely on details and guessing? Is he to learn the letters and their meanings by writing the letters and their meanings, by writing the letters down as they occur in the words he has himself selected from his own wide-ranging speaking vocabulary? This second solution has the advantage of making the child personally involved, but it has the disadvantage of asking him to learn many sound-meanings for single symbols. Or is he to have a vocabulary specially selected to help him understand the relationship between the sounds he speaks and the letters he writes? This means a selection of regularly phonic words with the disadvantage that a great deal of the child's own vocabulary must be cut out, but it has the advantage of giving him confidence in his ability to work things out for himself and probably also the subtle advantage of enabling the ear to help the eye. Because there is a constant relationship between the visual symbol (the printed letter) and the aural symbol (part of the *spoken* word) it is likely the inter-relationship between the senses being so close that the one sense will help the other and he will both hear better and see better. This is the crucial stage, the stage of really learning to read.

(f)   There is the stage which all readers of this book have reached of being so familiar with the printed word that they can read a whole book, every word in it if they care, without seeing more than a part of it in the ordinary sense of the word *see*. They tell themselves what they are going to see and therefore see it—as, for example, it is unnecessary to pay any attention to the first word on a page if the preceding page ended with the words . . .

The Queen waved from the balcony of Buckingham

. . . This is the stage of full and fluent silent reading, the stage of seeing without looking. Great efforts are being made in some industries to speed up the reading of executives by training them to see more at a glance, widening the eye-span. Better results would be achieved if it were more fully realised that it is not so much a matter of widening the eye-span as of increasing the brain-reach, by increasing the amount of information received from reduced retinal clues.

These then are the stages. It should be noted, however, that no one leaves any stage entirely behind. Printed words are often in our retinal images without our being conscious of them and whenever a new word comes our way as happened with *sputnik* we all go back to the letter-by-letter sounding-out or thinking-out method of the learning-to-read days, only it happens so quickly we are scarcely aware of it.

At the present time no official body anywhere in the English-speaking word supports any method of teaching reading which gives supremacy to letters. Anyone who says letters are important at the early stages of reading is thought to be advocating a return to methods long discredited, for it is assumed that they advocate the teaching of letters and letter-sounds right from the start. They do not necessarily mean that. What they may mean, and what J. C. Daniels and I do mean, is that the teacher and the designer of reading-books is gravely at fault if he does not accept the nature of alphabetic writing which dictates that the difference between a person who can read and one who cannot is that one knows the meanings of letters and the other does not.

For the English-speaking world these facts are of particular importance. It is very frequently given as a reason for adopting whole-words method that English is too irregular in its spelling for phonics to work. But the irregularity of English is the very reason which makes a phonic choice of teaching material important. With a regularly spelt language word-whole methods as practised in schools, with incidental phonics, offer no special difficulties.

English has become the international language of science. Considerable amounts of public money have been voted for 'the sale' of English to foreign parts. Yet the world is flooded with books for teaching the reading of English as though it had not an alphabet. Tomorrow, perhaps, or the next day, some government body somewhere will wake up to the fact that in the war of ideas the English-speaking world is fighting with one hand tied behind its back.

Chapter XVII

LAST WORDS

This book has dealt in detail with one main aspect of teaching reading. I have only by implication touched upon the emotional life of the child which in these days has rightly received a great deal of attention.

An unhappy or insecure home background seriously affects a child's progress at school—not in reading alone. In such cases a teacher by her sympathy and understanding can do something to help the child, but can do nothing about the root cause.

Yet not all emotional disturbances are caused by the home environment. Again and again teachers have reported that when a child backward in reading achieves success after a course of remedial treatment the child's whole personality undergoes a change. There is indeed a good reason for thinking that many emotional disturbances are due to the frustration which comes when a child who has enjoyed his 'pseudo-reading' is suddenly called upon to do some real reading.

Terman and Walcutt, writing about the child whose reading is retarded because of such a false start, have this to say:

> He has learned to recognise a number of words by sight in his primer. So long as his memory keeps up with the words that he has to know he is successful and adjusted. But when the new words come faster than he can remember them, or, more typically, when the phonic clues that are introduced interfere with the habits of

word-recognition he is employing . . . then he sulks, he withdraws into himself, may hate school, fear his teachers, and quarrel with his school-mates. The real trouble is that he is confronted with new demands which he is not capable of meeting. He can't make the required discriminations; he is forced to work at a problem with no solution and is punished for failure. If the frustration reaches a certain point, the child ceases to try, and the deterioration of both his reading and his personal adjustment may from that point be very rapid.

When this sort of child is trained in phonics by an experienced remedial teacher, so that he gets the reading KEY and suddenly finds himself, his emotional problems disappear as if by magic. Dr. Orton has pointed out that the typical disturbed children with reading difficulties were happy and well-adjusted before the reading problem arose. Fernald has made the same observation. Successful remedial teachers report again and again that the greatest reward in their work is seeing the unhappy maladjusted child begin to gain confidence, open up, and forget his fears. But if the emotional disturbance had preceded the reading difficulty and therefore caused it, it would not disappear merely because the reading problem was corrected.

These words were written about children in America. So far educational psychology has neither asserted nor attempted to prove that American children are basically different from children in the rest of the English-speaking world. American methods are on the whole somewhat different from English methods, but the difference where it exists is one imposed upon current theory by teachers in English schools and, if there are fewer children here of the kind described, the credit of it cannot be placed to the account of the theory of perception critically examined in this book.

APPENDICES

Appendix I

VOCABULARIES OF READING BOOKS

When word-whole theory was applied to the design of reading-books, the "few-and-frequent" principle of vocabulary selection had to be evolved. The criterion of efficiency of a reading primer came to be: how few different words are there in it and how often are they repeated? If the teaching of reading is, however, accepted as being the teaching of letter-meanings, or "letters in action", then a different criterion of efficiency must be adopted. The idea of the traditional phonic method was to teach children the letters which they would then build up into words. Often there was too little attention to word-meanings in the matter so designed, and certainly too little attention to the linguistic experience of the child. On the other hand the word-whole books which were in theory closely linked to the child's experience of the spoken word were in fact cut off from the child's vocabulary through the necessity for cutting down the number of words used and for using the remaining few as frequently as possible. Briefly the difference between the two types of book was that in the phonic books the number of letter-meanings the child had to learn was controlled while in the word-whole books it was the number of different words that was controlled.

With such points as these in mind some of the reading-schemes best-known in England were analysed in respect of (a) the number of different words used at the early stages, (b) the number of different letter-meanings in those words. The vocabulary of the first book in each scheme was taken, although in the case of the *Royal Road Readers*, only Part 1 of Book 1 was taken, this being in the current edition of these readers a book in itself.

In each case, except *Beacon*, the words are listed, reading down the columns, in the order of their first occurrence. The *Beacon* list is given in alphabetic order because it is expected that the children will not be meeting these words in the book until they have had considerable experience of these particular words in their printed form through the use of flash-cards and various word-involving activities which are an integral part of the scheme.

BEACON (Ginn & Co. Ltd.):

a	horse	read
and	I	Rover
baby	is	run
ball	it	Ruth
can	John	see
catch	kitty	sister
come	like	the
do	little	to
dog	me	too
has	mother	will
feed	my	with
have	play	yes
his	pretty	you

Number of different words: 39.

Number of different letter-meanings: 45.

$$\frac{\text{Words}}{\text{Letter-meanings}} \cdot 86$$

Number of phonically simple words: 11.

Number of irregular words: 28.

CHELSEA READERS (Harrap):

a	top	sat
man	mop	gas
cap	on	peg
cat	the	pet
pot	sun	fat
pan	gum	pug
tap	gun	Sam
can	dot	did
mat	sum	not
cot	dog	kiss

APPENDIX

tin	red	bed
cut	my	fox
in	fan	as
is	hen	at
it	big	well
pat	hat	bun
dig	egg	box
pig	had	buzz
dug	rag	has
pit	jam	hit
get	mug	his
pup	of	hut
pin	bat	bag
jug	doll	Sid
		got

Number of different words: 73.

Number of letter-meanings: 28.

$$\frac{\text{Words}}{\text{Letter-meanings}} \quad 2\cdot 6$$

Number of phonically simple words: 72.

Number of irregular words: 1.

GAY WAY (Macmillan):

the	in	on
big	little	Meg
red	tin	had
lorry	to	no
went	top	house
up	bang	is
the	ting	live
hill	a	I
pots	fell	will
and	down	go
pans	it	Jip

iv

cat	so	Deb
who	Sam	rat
are	fox	fat
you	run	pig
am	Ben	sat
can	dog	of

Number of different words: 51.

Number of letter-meanings: 43.

$$\frac{\text{Words}}{\text{Letter-meanings}} \quad 1 \cdot 2$$

Number of phonically simple words: 33.

Number of irregular words: 18.

HAPPY VENTURE (Oliver and Boyd):

here	the	sits
is	and	by
Dick	this	ball
Nip	in	big
Dora	mud	it
Fluff	fell	fun
a	can	play
dog	you	Jack
I	wet	bring
see	am	will
run	cat	get
to	tree	not
Jane	with	she
has	mother	take

Number of different words: 42.

Number of letter-meanings: 47.

$$\frac{\text{Words}}{\text{Letter-meanings}} \quad \cdot 9$$

Number of phonically simple words: 22.

Number of irregular words: 20.

JANET AND JOHN (Nisbet):

Janet	dog	I
John	run	two
come	here	three
look	down	play
and	up	go
see	aeroplane	jump
the	my	can
boats	one	horse
little	kitten	ride

Number of different words: 27.

Number of letter-meanings: 44.

$$\frac{\text{Words}}{\text{Letter-meanings}} \quad \cdot 6$$

Number of phonically simple words: 7.

Number of irregular words: 20.

MCKEE READERS (Nelson):

Tip	me	ball
no	with	play
here	Susan	will
come	find	you
Peter	home	and
is	go	the
not	I	

Number of different words: 20.

Number of letter-meanings: 35.

$$\frac{\text{Words}}{\text{Letter-meanings}} \quad \cdot 6$$

Number of phonically simple words: 5.

Number of irregular words: 15.

APPENDIX

ROYAL ROAD READERS (Chatto and Windus):

cat	sun	has
man	hen	his
pig	bib	hand
hat	lid	hut
jam	lad	hill
nib	mug	smell
bat	pin	rabbit
van	whip	lost
ink	spotted	fog
cup	jumped	spilt
dog	limped	flag
net	banged	flap
log	drum	wind
bus	milkcan	well
fox	when	kilt
bed	cracked	jug
rod	bull	crab
web	rat	just
Tom	leg	bitten
Ann	sand	big
stand	nest	kilt
sit	on	kit
run	at	grass
a	egg	raft
the	up	gull
top	is	mask
tap	not	full
tin	stop	glass
tub	Sam	yes
pan	dig	no
pot	in	lamp
pod	fan	fill
cot	fat	bag
dot	rug	caravan
mop	and	cliff
nun	fast	invalid
nut	as	rest
bin	fit	umbrella
bud	hot	kitten

basket	sack	milkman
duck	back	bring
stick	wicket	milk
six	Texas	plank
stumps	print	staff
swim	ring	lift
pond	king	cannot
lick	wing	strong
gum	tongs	rock
stamp	rung	bucket
		pond

Number of different words: 148.
Number of letter-meanings: 30.

$$\frac{\text{Words}}{\text{Letter-meanings}} \quad 4 \cdot 9$$

Number of phonically simple words: 137.
Number of irregular words: 11.

VANGUARD READERS (Macdougall):

Tom	Bob	table
Ann	jump	have
and	Tib	a
run	hop	ball
walk	can	play
to	sit	come
Baby	on	me
Mother	the	dog
this	chair	cat
is	my	us
Father	stand	am
I	you	garden
see	window	go
here	at	school
		do

Number of different words: 43.
Number of letter-meanings: 47.

$$\frac{\text{Words}}{\text{Letter-meanings}} \quad \cdot 9$$

Number of phonically simple words: 20.
Number of irregular words: 23.

Appendix II

PERCEPTION AND SPELLING

Teachers frequently suggest that word-whole methods produce poor spellers. Junior school teachers in particular seem to be of that opinion. On the other hand there are some teachers who hold the opposite point of view and suggest that poor ability in spelling goes along with a phonic method of learning to read. The argument in this case is that, having learned to read phonically simple words, a child is likely to give a phonically simple spelling to words which are not conventionally spelt in that way—to write "no" instead of "know", for example.

There are to my knowledge no controlled investigations which one could quote as decisive on this topic. There are some pointers, however. For example, Walcutt has pointed out that pupils in some American schools which have in recent years switched to phonics score four or five years above the national normal in spelling.

There are many educational topics, however, about which one can write with point and cogency without being able to quote precise figures—and this is one of them.

Although words may be the units of speech and words and phrases the units of accomplished reading the letter is the unit of writing, typing and printing. There is only one way of spelling correctly—putting the right letters in the right order. The fact that "knowledge" begins with k is of no importance in speech. There, the letter k has indeed no significance whatsoever in speech, but in writing (i.e. spelling) this letter has exactly the same importance as every other one in the word.

The pupil who recognises "pig" merely by its shortness and the dot on the "i" will not be able to spell even that simple word, nor will a pupil who cannot see the difference between "ocvcglomc" and "aeroplane" be able to spell "aeroplane".

Part-seeing at the early stages may take a pupil some way in reading, but can take him nowhere in spelling. On the other hand, as we have seen, the pupil who can really read has a knowledge of letters, and it may be that whether a pupil can spell well or not at the early stages is of no importance at all. The really pertinent question may be not whether at, say, the age of seven a pupil is an atrocious speller of the comparatively few words he tries to write, but whether the manner of his introduction to reading has delayed effects upon his spelling ability at the age of eleven or later. It is difficult, however, to see how this question could be answered in scientific terms. And there is a whole batch of subsidiary questions which are equally difficult to answer.

Does the use of introductory reading material in the design of which the significance of letters is ignored develop in pupils a persistent habit of inaccurate perception which interferes with learning to spell?

Are pupils taught by a phonic method more adventurous in their use of words in written work than pupils who have less knowledge of letters, and do they therefore produce more spelling errors than less adventurous pupils who are likely to limit themselves to words they are familiar with in the written or printed form?

Does the "creative writing" method of teaching reading produce poor spellers because the pupils have to deal with all the complexities of English spelling at one and the same time?

To those questions there is at present no definite answer. Nevertheless the theory of perception put forward in this book has, I think, an important bearing on the teaching of spelling, and suggests a rather new approach to the question.

The main aim of all education, it seems to one, is to give pupils as much insight as possible into the workings of their own minds. As far as possible they should understand what they are doing and why they are doing it. Teaching pupils to do sums, for example, in a mechanical way may be efficient *instruction* but it is not *education* in the real sense of the term. Teaching them to *understand* the properties of numbers and the processes of arithmetic, however, belongs to education not to mere instruction, though the instruction may well be improved because of the understanding that has been imparted. It is perhaps difficult to think of anything a pupil has to learn in school which belongs so completely to instruction as the teaching of spelling does and has so slender a connection with education. One could, of course, build up a mystique about spelling, linking orthography with etymology, but it is very doubtful if the practical results achieved thereby would repay the time and energy expended, nor would the understanding of the written language be improved to a degree that would justify this approach in preference to others.

There is a certain minimum set of facts about written language which a pupil ought to know in an articulate way, however. He ought to know the two main facts which the experts on reading have so consistently neglected during the past few decades: (*a*) that letters or letter-combinations have a meaning in that they convey instructions about which sounds we are to make in speech (*b*) that the order in which these letters or letter-combinations are set down on the page signifies an order in time.

Knowing these facts, the child is in possession of reasons why a vast number of words are spelt as they are. These facts are so exceedingly simple that one might think they do not need to be pointed out. Any child who can really read, it might be thought, knows them. This is not so. I have known children, fluent readers, who were not sufficiently alive to the significance of these facts to be able to put them into words.

What is even more to the point from the *educational* point of view is the possibility of giving the child some understanding of his own perpetual processes. The simple experiments in perception described in this book are very easy to carry out in the classroom. The close relationship between what one says to oneself and what one sees can be strikingly brought over even to pupils in the upper junior school by means of these experiments. A great many spelling mistakes are due not to ignorance of how a word should be spelt but to inability to see what is on the page, because of knowledge of the context. The pupil who has seen demonstrated the fact that the eyes can be deceived by what one says to oneself, who has himself been caught out seeing a complete word when it was not there in complete form, will be better able to understand why he has to be extremely careful to the extent of ignoring the meaning of words when he is checking the spelling. More than that, such a pupil is not only better equipped technically for dealing with spelling mistakes he has also acquired greater insight into the working of his own mind.

Appendix III

A NOTE ON ERRORS IN READING

The commonest cause of error in reading is that which was described in *Progress in Reading* as "part-seeing and whole-saying" when the pupil says the first word that comes into his head, as it were, after having perceived only part of the printed word in front of him. Bennett put this as follows: "A pronounced characteristic of pupils retarded in word-recognition seems to be the tendency not to inhibit associated responses until a word is clearly seen in all its parts—beginning, middle and end".

It is noticeable that the letters most clearly seen are the beginning and end letters—presumably because they stand out against the adjacent white spaces. Woodworth speaks of the "masking" effect of the other letters upon one another.

The following short list of errors is given not only for its intrinsic interest, but also so that the reader may amuse himself by deducing reasons for these mis-readings.

ask	sat, slack, that's.
at	it, that, as.
baby	bath, boys.
beautiful	butterfly.
black	back, make, bath, book.
come	came, me.
get	gate, lot.
high	hide, night, hand, had, fire, like.
little	letter.
two	toy, cow, town.
walked	walk, wall, work, want.
with	will, what, wit, like, is.

BIBLIOGRAPHY

BIBLIOGRAPHY

BETTS, E. A. .. .. Foundations of Reading Instruction with Emphasis on Differentiated Guidance. (*American Book Co.*, 1950).

BOARD OF EDUCATION .. Report of the Consultative Committee on Infant and Nursery Schools. (1933).

BOND, G. L. and .. .. Reading Difficulties, their Diagnosis and Cor-
TINKER, M. A. .. .. rection. (*Appleton-Century-Crofts*, 1957).

BOYCE, E. R. .. .. Learning to Read. (*Macmillan*, 1949).

DALE, NELLIE .. .. Further Notes on the Teaching of English Reading. (*Philip & Son*, 1902).

DANIELS, J. C. and .. Progress in Reading. (*University of Nottingham
DIACK, H. .. .. Institute of Education*, 1956).

Royal Road Readers: Teacher's Book. (*Chatto and Windus, 2nd Edition*, 1959).

Standard Reading Tests. (*Chatto and Windus*, 1958).

DEWEY, J. .. .. .. The School and Society. (*Maclure, Philips, New York*, 1900).

The Child and the Curriculum. (Rep. *University of Chicago*, 1956).

DOLCH, E. W. .. .. Problems in Reading. (*Garrard Press*, 1948).

Methods in Reading. (*Garrard Press*, 1955).

BIBLIOGRAPHY

DOWNES, L. W. and MURRAY, W.	..	Children Learn to Read: the play-way approach. (*Harrap*, 1955).
DUNCAN, J... ..	..	Backwardness in Reading: remedies and prevention. (*Harrap*, 1953).
ELLIS, W. D. ..	..	A Source-Book of Gestalt Psychology. (*Routledge & Kegan Paul*, 1938).
FLESCH, R.	..	Why Johnny Can't Read. (*Harper*, 1955).
FRANK, H.	..	A comparative study of children who are backward in reading and beginners in the infant school. (*British Journal of Educational Psychology*, Vol. 5, *p.l.*, 1955).
GATES, A. I... ..	..	The Improvement of Reading: a programme of diagnostic and remedial methods. (*Macmillan Co., New York*, 1947).
GIBSON, J. J. ..	..	The Perception of the Visual World. (*Allen & Unwin*, 1950).
GODDARD, N. L. ..	..	Reading in the Modern Infants' School. (*University of London Press*, 1959).
GRAY, W. S. ..	..	On Their Own in Reading. (*Scott Foresman*, 1948).
HAMAIDE, A. ..	..	The Decroly Class. (*Dent*, 1925).
HAMLYN, D. W. ..	..	The Psychology of Perception. (*Routledge & Kegan Paul*, 1957).
HUEY, E. B. ..	..	The Psychology and Pedagogy of Reading. (*Macmillan Co., New York*, 1908).
KATZ, D.	..	Gestalt Psychology. (*Methuen*, 1951).
KÖHLER, W... ..	..	Principles of Gestalt Psychology. (*Routledge & Kegan Paul*, 1935).
		The Mentality of Apes. (*Routledge & Kegan Paul*, 1927).
		Physical Gestalten. (General Problems, Selection 3 *in* Ellis, W. D., q.v.).
LASHLEY, K. S., CHOW, K. C. and SEMMES, J.		"An Examination of the Electrical Field Theory of Cerebral Integration". (*Psychology Rev.*, 1951).

xvi

BIBLIOGRAPHY

LEWIS, M. M. .. .. Infant Speech: A Study of the Beginnings of Language. (*Routledge & Kegan Paul, 2nd Edition*, 1951).

MINISTRY OF EDUCATION .. Reading Ability. (*H.M.S.O.*, 1950). Language. (*H.M.S.O.*, 1954).

MORRIS, C. .. .. .. Signs, Language and Behavior. (*Prentice-Hall, New York*, 1949).

MORRIS, J. .. .. .. Reading in the Primary School. (*Newnes*, 1959).

PETERMANN, B. .. .. The Gestalt Theory and the Problem of Configuration. (*Routledge & Kegan Paul*, 1932).

RUSSELL, D. H. .. .. Children Learn to Read. (*Ginn, Boston*, 1949).

SCHONELL, F. J. .. .. Backwardness in the Basic Subjects. 4th Edition. (*Oliver & Boyd*, 1948).

The Psychology of Teaching Reading. (*Oliver & Boyd*, 1945).

SMITH, N. B. .. .. American Reading Instruction. (*Silver, Burdett & Co.*, 1934).

TERMAN, S. and .. .. Reading: Chaos and Cure. (*McGraw-Hill*, 1958).
WALCUTT, C. C.

TRANSVAAL DEPARTMENT OF The Global Reading Method. (1955).
EDUCATION

VERNON, M. D. .. .. The Experimental Study of Reading. (*Cambridge U.P.*, 1931).

Visual Perception. (*Cambridge U.P.*, 1937).

A Further Study of Perception. (*Cambridge U.P.*, 1952).

Backwardness in Reading: A Study of its Nature and Origin. (*Cambridge U.P.*, 1957).

WERTHEIMER, M. .. .. Productive Thinking. (*Harper*, 1945).
Various papers as referred to in the text and published in Ellis's *Source-Book* (q.v.).

WITTY, P. .. .. .. Reading in Modern Education. (*Heath*, 1949).

xvii

INDEX

INDEX

Afrikaans, 153
alphabet, *see* letters
alphabetic method, 52 *et seq.*
'analogue', 39 *et seq.*
analysis:
    aural, 112
    visual, 80
'and-summation', 16
Anderson, I., 54, 62, 63, 75
Arnold, M., 49
associationist psychology, 16, 22
'atomistic' thinking, 16
attention, 41

Backwardness in Reading (Duncan), 16
Backwardness in Reading (Vernon), 85
Backwardness in the Basic Subjects (Schonell), 12, 82
battledores, 52
Barry, W. D., 56
Betts, E. A., 13, 54
Bond, G. F., 69
Boyce, E. R., 83, 111
British Journal of Educational Psychology, 139
Bruce and Barbara readers, 133
Bumstead, J., 55, 132
Burroughs, G. F. R., 112

Cattell, J. McK., 15, 62, 75, 81
Caxtons, The (Lytton), 53
'centre of interest', 65
Child and the Curriculum, The (Finlay), 64
children:
    linguistic development, 42 *et seq.*
    perceptual development, 43 *et seq.*, 86 *et seq.*
    speech vocabularies, 111 *et seq.*
    stages in reading development, 150
    under-fives attending school, 60
Children Learn to Read (Russell), 70
Chinese, English taught like, 135
Comenius, 12
configuration, 12
    of words, 70, 108
Cuisenaire, G., 61

Dale, N., 56, 59
Daniels, J. C., 120, 131
Dearborn, W. F., 54
Decroly, O., 65 *et seq.*

Dewey, J., 64
Dick and Jane readers, 133
Dickens, C., 60
Dodge, R., 76, 81
Dolch, E. W., 88
Drei Abhandlungen zur Gestalt Theorie (Wertheimer), 26
Duncan, J., 12, 89

education:
    and Gestalt theory, 49 *et seq.*
    of young children, 60
Ehrenfels, C. von, 15
Elementary English, 54
Ellis, W. D., 16, 19
England, reading in, 49, 53, 56 *et seq.*, 143 *et seq.*
Erdmann, B., 76, 81
errors in reading, 139 *et seq.*
experience:
    Gestalt, neglect of, 18 *et seq.*
    ambiguity of term, 22
experience theory, 22

Farnham, G. L., 64, 72, 132
'few and frequent' principle, 116 *et seq.*, 146
'field excitation', 17
field psychology, 34
figure-ground hypothesis, 33
Finlay, J. J., 64
First Companion Books (Daniels & Diack), 121
Flesch, R., 55, 135, 146
Foundations of Reading Instruction (Betts), 12
Frank, H., 139
Freud, A., 50
Freud, S., 50
Froebel, F., 60
Froebel Society, 60
Further Study of Perception, A (Vernon), 30

Gagg, J. C., 119, 125
Gates, A. I., 70, 72, 74, 82, 108
Gestalt:
    applied to reading, 12, 62, 67
    difficulty of defining, 16 *et seq.*
    physical, 17
    the printed word as a Gestalt, 51
    Wertheimer's definition, 15
Gestalt Psychology (Köhler), 25
Gestalt-qualitat, 15